Management for Professionals

For further volumes:
http://www.springer.com/series/10101

Jorij Abraham

Product Information Management

Theory and Practice

 Springer

Jorij Abraham
Ecommerce Foundation
Duivendrecht
The Netherlands

ISSN 2192-8096   ISSN 2192-810X (electronic)
ISBN 978-3-319-04884-0   ISBN 978-3-319-04885-7 (eBook)
DOI 10.1007/978-3-319-04885-7
Springer Cham Heidelberg New York Dordrecht London

Library of Congress Control Number: 2014938033

Printed on acid-free paper

Springer is part of Springer Science+Business Media (www.springer.com)

For Martine, Max & Mark.

Preface

I have worked for companies as a consultant on e-commerce issues for over a decade, and, more importantly, the driving force behind the success of e-commerce, Product Information Management (PIM).

During this period I learned the hard way what well set-up PIM processes and systems can do and (should) not do and how to select, implement and maintain such a system successfully (or otherwise).

With this book I hope to pass on some of these (painful) lessons learned, as follows:
- An overview of the benefits and opportunities of PIM;
- Knowledge about the key concepts of how PIM systems are set up;
- Insights into the different PIM processes and the possibilities offered by PIM;
- Information on how to select a PIM system which best meets your needs;
- Tips on how to circumvent technical pitfalls and make your PIM processes and system work.
- Advice on how to integrate PIM into your organization and build a PIM team.
  I have tried to write this book with different readers in mind:
- Managers, business users and students who need to be aware of what PIM can do;
- Project managers and technicians who have the good fortune or otherwise to have been selected to implement a PIM system;
- PIM users who need inspiration and guidelines on how to further improve and enhance their PIM system;
- Software vendors whose PIM systems already add enormous benefits but which could add so much more if further improved.
  Why did I write this book? Well, among other reasons:
- The importance of PIM is underestimated and companies should become more aware of its short-term operational benefits and its long-term strategic importance.
- There is no book on the market that really describes in detail PIM processes and systems, how to select and implement a PIM system and how to make it successful.
- A lot of (dis)information is available on the Internet and most of it is commercial and does not go into any real detail.
- I like to flatter my ego, and see my name come up next time you do a Google search for Product Information Management...

I received a lot of help from many different sources. Most importantly I would like to thank my family and friends who accepted that I was not always there when I should have been.

I would also very graciously like to express my gratitude to my former colleagues at Unic (see also the appendix about Unic and how Unic can help you with your e-commerce and PIM-related challenges) and in particular Marc Degen, Chris Jobse, Alexander Oppel, Maximilian Plank, Kay Puffer, Daniel Risch and Gerrit Taaks who helped me with their considerable expertise and feedback.

I would also like to thank all the e-commerce and/or PIM managers who shared with me their practical experience and insights. I would especially like to thank Dirk de Bruijn and Marisa Boselie (Beter Bed), Roman Desponds (Coca Cola HBC), Kees Heddes (CRH), Mark Mansier (De Bijenkorf), Angelique Vervloet and Peter Beekmans (Fabory Group), Alain Stopnicer (Manor), Laurent Christen (Nikon Europe), Nicolas Schibler (PKZ/The Look), Gijs van Wanrooy and Loes Kamerman (PVG) and Enri Meijers (Thomas Cook).

Finally, a large number of PIM software vendors have openly given insights into their systems and product strategy. This takes courage for which I am very grateful.

Duivendrecht, The Netherlands   Jorij Abraham

Contents

What Is PIM?

1.1   The Rise of PIM

Product Information Management (PIM) is a relatively new term. The concept started to gain momentum around 2003.

Its popularity is rising due, to a considerable extent, to the rapid growth of e-commerce and the popularity of online stores. First of all, selling online required companies to collect **clear basic product information** that consumers can actually understand. Without product information e.g. the name of the product, price and product category, the product could not be found and sold online at all.

Secondly, the Internet allows retail and wholesale companies to **offer many more products** online to their clients, often described as "**long tail**", than in physical stores.[1] While it was possible to manage product information for up to a thousand or more products in a spreadsheet, most online stores now offer tens if not hundreds of thousands of products. In this case spreadsheets simply no longer work.

In addition, product information is no longer offered via the Web but via a **large collection of channels** such as mobiles, tablets, stores, point of sale, printed catalogs, flyers, etc. This growth **demands** a **specialized system** to manage so much information so widely distributed.

At the same time **consumers demand more, better and consistent product information**. In general, the more information, the more you sell as clearly illustrates (we will prove this in Sect. 2.3.1) (Fig. 1.1).

A **detailed product description** is rated as one of the **most important features** of a Web shop (see Fig. 1.2). To sell a product online customers want to search and compare numerous details and want to know all the specifications before they buy.

---

[1] The long tail is, among other things, a retailing strategy of selling a large number of items with relatively small quantities of each sold—usually in addition to selling fewer popular items in large quantities. While retailers and wholesalers were in the last century forced to keep most of their products in stock in order to sell them, the Internet allows them to offer a much larger assortment and only order from their suppliers when they themselves have sold the product.

J. Abraham, *Product Information Management*, Management for Professionals, DOI 10.1007/978-3-319-04885-7_1, © Springer International Publishing Switzerland 2014

Fig. 1.1 Where would you shop? Customers demand more product information (*Source*: Heiler)

Likewise, they no longer accept a fuzzy picture but want high resolution photos, videos and 3D models.

Some examples of information customers demand of a product:

• Mattress: How many turns the springs in the mattress make;
• Fasteners: the surface treatment of a bolt;
• Dress: the exact circumference in centimeters of a dress at each 5 cm interval.

With the rise of more and more channels, customers demand that all this product information is consistently available across all channels.

However, there are also other trends that can explain the rise of PIM. For one, more and more **products are becoming information**. People buy tickets, download games and buy digital books and training courses online. To buy these virtual products customers want to have information in the form of photos, demos, videos, product reviews by other buyers and much more, before they buy.

A fourth reason is that companies are **legally obliged** to store more information about their products. Where are the materials source? How was the product manufactured? To which intermediaries was it sold? etc.

Finally, the world of distribution and selling of products is becoming **more complex**. Companies have seen the number of **customer segments** they distinguish becoming smaller and smaller, in the end **moving towards 1 to 1**. These customers use multiple channels (e.g. stores, the Web, mobile, catalogs, etc.). Companies have **multiple brands** across multiple **countries** with multiple **price lists** and **promotions** and are working with **thousands of suppliers**. The complexity of this world can no longer be managed without advanced processes and systems like PIM.

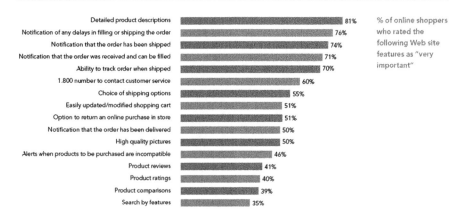

Detailed product descriptions — 81%
Notification of any delays in filling or shipping the order — 76%
Notification that the order has been shipped — 74%
Notification that the order was received and can be filled — 71%
Ability to track order when shipped — 70%
1.800 number to contact customer service — 60%
Choice of shipping options — 55%
Easily updated/modified shopping cart — 51%
Option to return an online purchase in store — 51%
Notification that the order has been delivered — 50%
High quality pictures — 50%
Alerts when products to be purchased are incompatible — 46%
Product reviews — 41%
Product ratings — 40%
Product comparisons — 39%
Search by features — 35%

% of online shoppers who rated the following Web site features as "very important"

Fig. 1.2 Product information is the most important feature for buying online (*Source*: Sterling Commerce, July 2007)

1.2   A Formal Definition

PIM actually stands for what it says it stands for: the management of product information.

Wikipedia gives the following definition[2]:

> Product information management or PIM refers to processes and technologies focused on centrally managing information about products, with a focus on the data required to market and sell the products through one or more distribution channels.

I agree with this definition. I do however want to further define the word "centrally". The end goal of PIM is to have one shared source of product information. However, this can also be set up in a distributed way as we will discuss in Sect. 7.7. The central concept however is that product information is entered and stored once. This place is the "single source of truth" (also called the "Golden Record") and from here that information is distributed without being re-entered manually into a different system.

---

[2] Source: http://en.wikipedia.org/wiki/Product_information_management

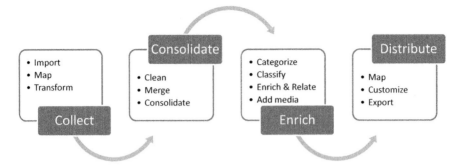

Fig. 1.3 PIM supports four main processes

In this book we will use the definition as used by Wikipedia as the basis to explain what PIM is, its benefits and how to implement its processes and systems.

1.3   Core Processes and Features (Fig. 1.3)

1.3.1   Collection

As product information is created across the organization and beyond, one of the primary tasks of PIM is to collect all this information. Product data is often stored in numerous different systems. According to a study by Heiler among 310 retailers and manufacturers, master data (e.g. product IDs, inventory and price) is stored in 3 to 20+ different systems at 48 % of the retailers and 88 % of the manufacturers researched.

As most information is stored in systems, most PIM systems have features to:
- **Import** data from **multiple sources** in **multiple formats** on a one time or interval basis (e.g. once per day, per hour);
- **Map** the imported **data** to specific product attributes;
- and if necessary **transform** this data to match the standards set (e.g. import the weight of a product of 15 ounces from a UK system to 0.4 kg in the central PIM system).

1.3.2   Consolidation

The ideal of PIM is to create **one single source of truth** for each product. One of the conditions for this is that the exact same product should only exist once in the system. It is often the case that the same products have been entered over the years numerous times by different employees under different names. Most PIM systems have mechanisms to prevent products from being entered more than once in the system.

Especially in large organizations which arose from mergers and acquisitions, merging double entries can be a tedious and lengthy manual process (see also see

Sect. 7.4 on data cleaning). Often it can only in part be supported by automated processes (like matching on external unique identifiers and just hope all parts of the organizations have used these in their systems).

Likewise, different content suppliers may provide different parts of the product information to be offered (e.g. suppliers A and B may both sell the same product where you may want to use the product title of supplier A and the product description of supplier B). Most PIM systems therefore have a selection of **tools to clean, merge and consolidate product information**.

1.3.3   Enrichment

The sources from which all product information has been gathered usually only contain basic facts about the product such as a unique product identifier, its purchase and selling price, weight and size. The sales and marketing departments want to add more information to the products to be able to sell them across different brands, channels, countries, etc. These departments want to add information about the unique qualities of the product, the durability for example and its ease of use.

In order to enrich products in a structured way all advanced PIM systems support **categorization and classification**. These concepts will be explained in more detail in Sect. 3.3. For now, categorization allows organizations to sort products into specific groups allowing a better overview of the entire assortment.

In addition, a **classification system** can help in the **management of attributes**. Attributes describe a specific element of a product such as its name, weight, height, length, width, etc. While it may sound superfluous to have a separate function to manage attributes, one of the basic concepts behind a PIM system is that it allows business users to add their own attributes to products without ICT support. In addition, management also becomes essential as the number of attributes can rise rapidly.

A commercially very interesting feature of PIM systems is the support of being able to **create relationships** between products. These relationships can be used for several purposes, including to:

• Show **similar** products to the product shown;
• **Up-sell** more expensive products;
• **Cross-sell** related accessories to a product;
• Explain that a product **consists of** multiple other products;
• Offer **spare parts** to a product;
• **Replace** an old product with a new product;
• Communicate that it is **mandatory** to buy another product with a particular product;
• Etc.

Most PIM systems in one way or another also allow users to add other media assets to a product other than attributes. Examples of media assets include **photos, video, manuals, CAD/CAM drawings**, etc.

These media assets are usually stored in a **Media Asset Management (MAM)** system which may be part of the PIM system or a separate module or system. Typical functions of a MAM system are the uploading and mass-importing of media assets, automatic assignment of media assets to categories and/or products, automatic resizing of photos and conversion of video for multiple distribution channels and adding meta data (e.g. device of capture, date of capture).

PIM systems have several features to **improve product data quality**:

- Automated data validation (e.g. preventing text from being entered in a field intended for a number);
- Verification for completeness (e.g. making sure that all mandatory fields are filled in);
- Version control makes sure revisions are kept and that the last version is always updated.

Data access control is the fifth enhancement feature that PIM systems support. As multiple users enter product information into the PIM system, mechanisms prevent the same user working on the same data at the same time. Access can also be limited to specific user groups, e.g. preventing users from editing products for which they are not responsible.

Finally, **workflow** allows the efficient organization of product enrichment. The enrichment of specific products can be assigned to specific users by a coordinator and when enrichment is done, a validation process can be initiated. A second benefit of workflow is that it makes it more transparent who has initiated which change and who has approved it. Workflow becomes essential particularly when product enrichment of the same product has to be done by different users (e.g. photographers and translators).

1.3.4 Distribution

PIM systems in themselves do not serve as publication channels. They can however export data in much the same way as they can import data. PIM systems can deliver data once, at regular intervals, or on request to different **channels** in **multiple formats**. Some example exports are:

- To a paper catalog via a nightly XML or CSV batch file.
- To a sales department via an ad hoc manual Excel file.
- To a Web site via a Web service on an ad hoc basis.

1.4   Who Uses a PIM System?

A PIM system has many different users. Excluding those who use the product information for reading purposes only (e.g. the different distribution channels discussed in the next section) nearly every department in an organization often uses the PIM system in one way or another.

The PIM system can in fact be used by the entire value chain:

- **Suppliers** may use it to add information about their products to customers' PIM systems or update their prices and inventory levels.
- The **procurement** department in an organization may use the PIM system to store gathered product information such as prices, but also product quality criteria and contracts as agreed upon with suppliers.
- The **R&D or design department** may use the system to store CAD/CAM drawings, technical specifications of parts and other technical documentation created in the product development process.
- **Marketing and sales** usually add more commercial information which helps customers make an informed choice or have a better product experience. This may be factual information but also glossy product photos.
- **Customer care:** may add complaints and frequently asked questions about the product which the product design department can use to improve the product itself or its documentation.
- **Customers:** may add product reviews and photos and videos of how they use the product in real life.

The actual number of users may differ widely per company. The number of viewers may be huge if one of the channels is the company Web site. However, usually only a small group of people in a separate **product information management unit** is actually involved in the day-to-day maintenance of the product information (see also Sect. 7.7). However, even this small group may add up to several hundreds of users if distributed across the entire value chain.

1.5   PIM's Position in the Enterprise

The sharp focus of PIM systems makes it clear that it is only one system of the many that an organization needs. However, when it comes to product information, the PIM system takes a central role between different sources of product information and the distribution channels to which the PIM exports its data, as Fig. 1.4 highlights.

1.5.1   Sources

A PIM can get its information from multiple sources. These sources may include:
- **ERP systems:** nearly every production, wholesale and retail organization has one or even multiple ERP systems to manage the logistical and financial processes within their organization. These systems are also usually the main source for all products the company offers. If a product does not exist in these systems, most organizations cannot even store, ship, let alone sell it. The product ID used in the ERP system is often also the unique identifier of the product in the PIM system. Likewise, the ERP usually remains the source of price information which may differ per country and customer (segment).

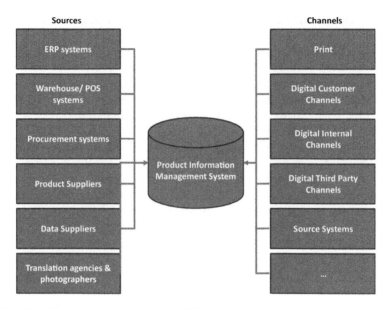

Fig. 1.4 Possible sources and channels of a PIM system

- **Warehouse/POS systems**: warehouse systems and Cash Registries (also called Till systems) often have a more accurate view of the actual, local, inventory of a product. A PIM is often used to create a central overview. ERP systems often also collect this information, but these systems are not suitable for collecting and distributing this information in real time.
- **Procurement systems**: these systems can typically provide the PIM with purchase prices and supplier data.
- **Product Suppliers**: suppliers of products cannot only deliver the actual products to a wholesaler or retailer but also the information that belongs to the products. Often the information suppliers can only provide basic data such as prices, weight and size dimensions but sometimes also commercial information such as product descriptions and photos. The number of suppliers can be significant as Fig. 1.5 from a study by Heiler shows. Two thirds of the participating companies reported having over 100 suppliers. 21 % of respondents even have more than 1,000 suppliers.
- **Data suppliers**: in several industries, such as travel and electronics, third parties exist that can offer product information. Often producers do not have or do not want to distribute product information and this role is taken on by a third party. Examples of third party data suppliers are C|Net (electronics), Touristiek (holiday destinations, hotels and accommodation) and Tradcom (industrial supplies). The data these suppliers provide is usually very rich and includes a considerable amount of commercial information relevant for (end-)customers and may include photo and video material. Parties like CNet and Touristiek also deliver customer product reviews.

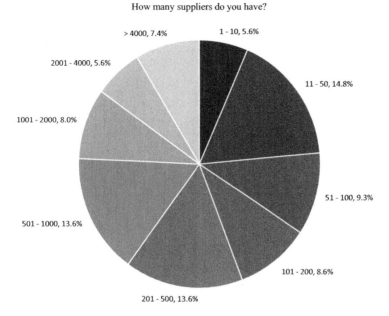

How many suppliers do you have?

Fig. 1.5 Number of suppliers manufacturers and retailers have (*Source*: Heiler)

- **Translation agencies and photographers**: Often translation and product photography are outsourced to external parties. These parties also provide data to the PIM systems by accessing the system externally or via more complex interfaces like file upload or Web services.

The number of sources a company may have differs widely. Often only integration with an ERP system is needed. However, larger organizations in particular can have over 20 sources of product information that must be integrated.

1.5.2 Channels

The number of communication, sales and distribution channels companies can use has expanded rapidly in the last two decades. In the past 5 years mobile phones and tablets have changed from being non-existent to important communication channels. Internet television and smartware (e.g. glasses and smart watches) are expected to gain in popularity over the next 3–5 years, together with voice-controlled applications like Siri, introduced by Apple.

As Fig. 1.6 shows, channels can be divided into physical channels and digital channels, and into channels owned by the organization itself and channels where it relies on third parties. All channels need product information to inform, sell, and distribute products.

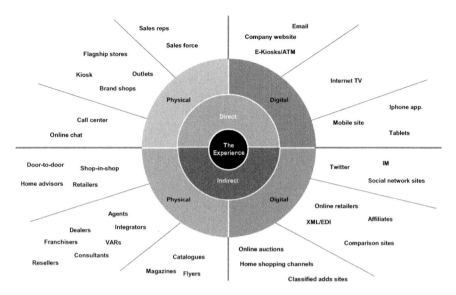

Fig. 1.6 The number of channels is always on the increase

Some of the most common channel groups a PIM system distributes its information to are:

- **Print**: although many believe that print is "dead". In practice this is not the case at all. Catalogs are still very popular in industries such as travel, wholesale and even retail. However, the big catalogs with boring product indexes are slowly being replaced by glossy magazines and flyers with attractive visual displays of product offerings. These print communications are also becoming more personalized to specific customer segments and will, in the end, be created based on the personal interests of the individual receiver. Chapter 5 discusses PIM and Print in more detail.
- **Digital customer channels**: be it the company Web site, email newsletter, mobile apps, or point of sale systems, the PIM system should be able to deliver product information targeted to the specific needs of the particular channel. For example, a PIM system should deliver a low resolution photo to a mobile channel and a high definition video to the Web, or competitor prices to sales staff' intranet, and unique buying reasons to consumers.
- **Digital internal channels**: wherever they are, employees need access to product information to better inform and sell to customers. Digital channels take a more explicit role in this as in-store sales staff can access product information via the till, call center agents have access to the company e-commerce system, and the sales force uses tablets to do the same.
- **Digital third party channels**: in the last decade companies like Amazon, eBay and other online marketplaces have become important sales channels. As these marketplaces are aware, they sell more with good product information, and they

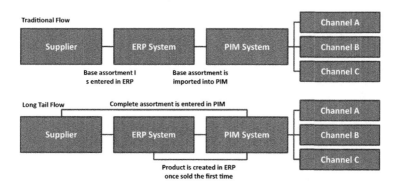

Fig. 1.7 The flow between the ERP and PIM system is changing

have started to demand more and better product information from their retailers. Similarly, the same companies have now started experimenting with placing product information on social media such as Facebook and LinkedIn.

- **Source systems**: these systems (e.g. ERP systems) cannot only function as a source for PIM systems but may also receive enriched information backup that can be used in the logistical and financial processes of the company. One example is a product photo imported into the ERP system from the PIM system so that that warehouse staff can validate the right product has been picked.
- **Data warehouses**: and other business intelligence tools often import data from PIM systems to support the analysis of products in store, advertised, sold, etc. Using product data can help identify trends e.g. which product categories are gaining in popularity, and which products can best be cross-sold with other products.

Nikon is an example of a company that uses its PIM system for several channels. The same data is used for a B2C Web site, a B2C mobile Web site, a B2B ordering platform and an employee intranet shop (see the Nikon Case for more information).

1.5.3   PIM Is Gaining Ground

PIM systems are becoming more important within the organization. Some companies are even changing the flow of information between the ERP and PIM system (see Fig. 1.7). These companies have started selling products from their PIM system without it being known in their ERP system. This allows them to offer entire ranges from their suppliers without polluting their ERP systems with products that are never sold (e.g. the long-tail effect as described in Sect. 1.1).

1.6   Related Systems

While PIM has only been around since about 2003, there are several systems that are comparable to or overlap with PIM.

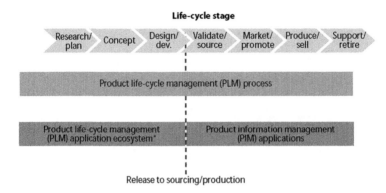

Fig. 1.8 Product lifecycle management and PDM and PIM (*Source*: Forrester, 2009)

1.6.1 Product Related Systems

PIM actually covers only part of the **Product Lifecycle Management (PLM)** process. The idea of PLM is that the entire lifecycle of a product from idea, through concept, prototype, first commercial version to the moment service and support is still provided after the product is no longer being sold, is supported and managed. Figure 1.8 outlines the difference visually.

In practice most PLM systems actually focus on the product development side, helping, among other areas, the project management of product development, creation of Bill of Material (BOM) lists, engineering change management, part traceability, quality management, etc.

Product Resource Management (PRM) and **Product Content Management (PCM)**: are used as **alternative terms for PIM**. The terms are more popular in certain countries (PCM is, for example, more commonly used in the USA than in Europe) and therefore also by specific software vendors.

While a PIM system focuses on the management of product information relevant for marketing and sales, **Product Data Management (PDM)** is aimed at supporting the development and manufacturing of products. Alternative names for PDM include PLM, EDM, CPDM, CPC, VPDM, PDM II, PLCM and E-PDM. PDM allows for the management of the enormous amount of information that comes with the creation of products: bills of materials, supplier contracts, parts specifications, CAD/CAM drawings, minutes of meetings, etc. All related information has to be stored for each version of a product. In addition, PDM systems can help in the classification of products (just like PIM systems), configuration management (how has the product changed over time) and visualization of products (often using plug-ins into external CAD/CAM systems). They often also have workflow functionality, just like PIM systems do (Könst et al. 2009).

Digital Asset Management (DAM) or Media Asset Management (MAM) support the processes and systems to manage photos, presentations, videos, documents, CAD/CAM drawings and other media and their related meta-information (authors, creation date, revisions, etc). DAM systems are often used by marketing departments to store all marketing-related media to create brochures, posters, catalogs and flyers. Most PIM systems offer (a light version of) a DAM as part of their proposition to store product-related media.

1.6.2   Content Related

Enterprise content management (ECM) can be seen as the overarching concept of managing all content related information within the organization and beyond. PIM is a sub entity of ECM, just like:
- **Content Management Systems (CMS)** for publishing, editing and modifying, often semi-structured, content, especially for internal and external Web sites.
- **Document management systems (DMS)** that are used to store documents and usually have features like version control and archiving.
- **Cross Media Publishing (CMP)** systems that originate from the publishing and advertising industry. They allow authors to create an article once and distribute it across multiple media like a Web site, magazine or mobile app.

1.6.3   Process Related

Enterprise Resources Planning (ERP) systems are usually an important source of product information for PIM systems. However, ERP systems focus on supporting operational processes like logistics and finance. While some ERP systems allow the management of product information, most were not set up with this in mind. Few support the key processes of a PIM or only with serious ICT effort involved.

Master Data Management (MDM) offers a central repository to manage business critical data on an ongoing basis. It is the linchpin between different operational systems and between these systems and systems used for data analysis. It allows master users, also called data stewards, to manage key data (customers, products, partners) that is shared across the organization in one system. Its key functions are data collection, cleaning, consolidation and distribution across systems.

Looking at the processes PIM and MDM support, they are, to some extent, much alike. However, their focus is very different. While MDM is responsible for harmonizing the core data of the company, including that of customers and suppliers, a PIM system focuses on extending and enhancing product data. An MDM is rarely used to enrich information but ensures that all systems in the enterprise can communicate with each other using the same data definitions.

For example, an MDM can create one view on a customer called "John Doe" by pulling data out of multiple systems (e.g. where system A may use as customer ID

"Doe, J." and system B "J.M. Doe"). Where the PIM system is the single source of truth for product information, the MDM is not a "source" system but a system that allows users to work across multiple systems by unifying data.

Reference

Könst, J. S., la Fontaine, J. P., & Hoogeboom, M. G. R. (2009, August). *Product data management, a strategic perspective*. Geldermalsen: Maj Engineering Publishing.

Benefits of a PIM System

2

While the theoretical benefits of a PIM system are numerous, building a business case to implement a PIM system proves, in practice, to be more difficult. It is even the primary reason why a PIM project cannot be started.

This chapter discusses the benefits of a PIM system on strategic, tactical and operational levels based on material from several research papers and our own case studies.[1]

2.1 Strategic Benefits

There are several strategic reasons for implementing PIM in the organization. The most common are:

2.1.1 Assortment Expansion

In Sect. 1.1 we briefly described the long-tail strategy some wholesalers and retailers follow. The benefits of a long-tail strategy are not only that more products can be sold to the same customers (and potential new ones as well) but also that the products in the long tail can be sold against a higher margin. As Fig. 2.1 shows, in general, price competition is much stronger for the top 20 % of the assortment than for the remaining 80 % of the assortment (the long tail). Aberdeen, for example,

---

[1] Among the research papers used are:
- A.T. Kearney, Action Plan to Accelerate Trading Partner Electronic Collaboration, Data Synchronization Proof of Concept: Case Studies from Leading Manufacturers and Retailers.
- The Yankee Group, The Cost of Waiting: Building the ROI Case to Implement Product Information Management Now, January 2005.
- Aberdeen Group, The Instant Power of All-Channel PIM: Increased Sales and Competitiveness, December 2011.

J. Abraham, *Product Information Management*, Management for Professionals,   15
DOI 10.1007/978-3-319-04885-7_2, © Springer International Publishing Switzerland 2014

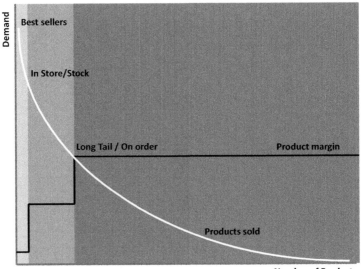

Fig. 2.1 Long-tail assortment has a higher product margin

reports up to 29 % higher profits due to higher product margins in the long-tail assortment.

In Fig. 2.2 we see a clear relationship with the size of a company's assortments and having a PIM system. It is remarkable to see that when the assortment increases to over one million SKUs there are no companies who do not have a PIM system. 38 % of the retailers with a PIM system stated that they were aiming to achieve an additional 50 % expansion in their assortment, while 45 % are planning to expand their product range by between 11 % and 50 % in the next 3 years. This figure was 20 % lower for retailers without PIM.

However, implementing a long-tail strategy entails much more than just adding an Excel sheet with data from a supplier to your PIM system.

Processes have to be set up to manage the information in the PIM system. Price mechanisms have to be set up to manage the margin for which products are sold. Just adding 30 % margin to all products might be a simple thing to do, but it does not take into consideration the actual logistical costs, perceived product value by the customer, and competitors' prices. Likewise, when suppliers stop selling a product, the product also has to be removed from the assortment of the wholesaler or retailer.

Once a product is sold, the product has to be ordered, possibly repackaged at the company's warehouse and delivered to the customer. To do this, logistical processes have to be set up in the ERP system, especially when the ERP system does not yet know the product just sold.

With the external and internal processes set up right, companies are able to expand their offering very fast. WarmteService for example was able to expand its

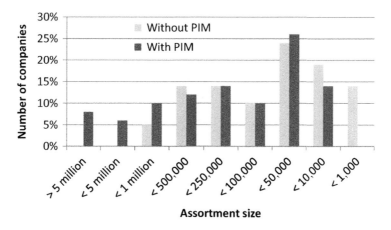

Fig. 2.2 Retailers with and without a PIM system in relation to their assortment size (*Source*: Heiler)

offering from 20,000 products to 150,000 products in less than 1.5 years (see the Warmteservice Case for more information).

2.1.2   Shorten Time to Market

Improvements in time to market have been recorded in several research papers. AT Kearney reports improvements of 7–13 % for wholesalers, while Aberdeen writes of a reduction by a factor of 10 for a software company.

A PIM system can reduce the time to market of a product significantly for producers in particular. If the PIM system is also used during the design process, it allows for the development and production across multiple locations, countries and time zones by multiple partners.

In addition, the commercial product information can already be created while the product is still being manufactured, or even being designed. Once set up well, the product information can already be distributed in an organized fashion, and sales can start exactly at the moment the product actually becomes available, or even earlier.

However, the effect also applies to wholesalers and retailers. With PIM set up, information can be distributed faster to all relevant channels across the globe to market and sell a product. This may be of strategic importance in a competitive environment where new products are being released all the time.

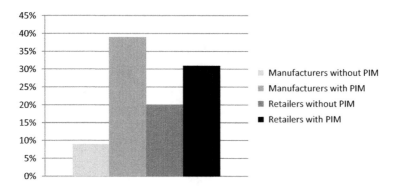

Fig. 2.3 Companies that stated to have very high-level customer satisfaction/loyalty

2.1.3 Uniform Customer Experience Across All Channels

However, the most important strategic benefit may be that a uniform customer experience can be created with a PIM system across all channels. Without PIM product information is managed per channel and will quickly lead to awkward results e.g. the use of two different product names for the same product in the wholesale and retail channels, and even disastrous differences e.g. inexplicable price differences (Fig. 2.3).

In the Heiler study, the manufacturers surveyed do indeed report a link between their performance in connection with product information quality as a result of using PIM and customer loyalty: 39 % of respondents confirm very high levels of customer satisfaction while only 9 % of those not using PIM rate their performance to be similarly high. For retailers, the difference between 31 % for those using PIM and 20 % for non-users is less, but nevertheless clear. Likewise, Yankee Group reports an increase of 26 % in customer loyalty due to the introduction of a PIM system.

2.2 Tactical Benefits

2.2.1 Manage Complexity

PIM allows companies to manage, and increase, the complexity of their organization. The number of dimensions in on the increase:
- Number of products;
- Number of attributes per product;
- Number of languages;
- Number of suppliers;
- Number of countries;
- Number of channels;

- Number of product localizations/customizations;
- Number of customer-specific assortments and prices;
- ...

Without a PIM system it would be impossible for a company like Fabory to manage 120,000 products, from 3,000 suppliers in 32 languages across 58 countries (see the Fabory Case). Complexity increases further as products may vary slightly per country due to local preferences (e.g. the color white has different meanings in different cultures—from celebration to death), or legislation (e.g. one component of a product may differ as different materials have to be used). We do not even consider the fact that more and more products are increasingly customized to meet customer-specific needs.

A PIM system would seem to be a prerequisite for working internationally. In the ROI study conducted by Heiler we see that manufacturers with a PIM system operate in over 45 countries, while manufacturers who do not have a PIM system are only represented in 17 countries. Manufacturers with a PIM system provide product information in 19 languages whereas non-PIM users only support 4 languages. This difference will only increase as manufacturers with a PIM system plan to add 8 more languages over the next 3 years while non-PIM manufacturers are planning only 1.

Heiler also discovered that organizations with a PIM system offer:

- Customer specific assortments to more customers,
- with per customer-specific assortment more products,
- and with more differentiation in product prices.

2.2.2 Controlled Content Distribution

A central PIM system gives companies more control over which external parties get which product information than old distribution media like CD-ROMs do.

Some producers have an active policy to provide preferred retailers with more and better product information earlier, while reducing the number of product attributes and resolution of product photos to less preferred distribution channels.

This is, for example, often the case in the travel industry where tour operators provide retailers with less content than on their own Web site. In this way they can distinguish their own Web site from retailers selling their own products to the same consumers.

2.2.3 Legal Compliance

Legal compliance is increasingly becoming an important tactical benefit. With registration of who edits which information and who approves which content, companies with a PIM system state to have up to 50 % better control over their data than companies without PIM.

2.3   Operational Benefits

2.3.1   Increased Turnover

It has been proven that the provision of good product information, improves sales. Studies have shown that online **conversion ratios** can increase from **17 % to 56 %**, according to AT Kearney, by providing better product information. Likewise, Aberdeen reports **16 %** more product sales by increased conversion rates in e-commerce.

Online conversion is increased in several ways:

- Online better **keyword search, navigation, filter and comparison facilities** can be offered when product information is in order.
    - **Keyword search** can be improved by limiting search results only to relevant categories and fields. A few examples:

        Products in the "Banana" category probably match the search term "banana" better than an apple with within its description "banana like taste".

        Similarly, PIM systems can support search by maintaining alternative names for products (e.g. a "Golden Kiwi" might also be called "Yellow Kiwi").

        Many PIM systems not only support alternative names for products but also categories and attributes. As a result, the query "banana like taste" can be translated to taste = banana which again might result in showing bananas as search result but also apples which have as value for taste "banana".

        Finally PIM systems store values separately from the unit they are specified in. A search for a "2 pound pineapple" can therefore result in showing pineapples with a weight index of 0.75–1.25 kg.
    - **Navigation** can be improved with clear categorization. E.g. most users will instinctively search for pineapples in the "Exotic fruit" category.
    - **Filtering** (also called facetted search) becomes possible when attributes are standardized, allowing users, for example, to filter on size (S, M, L, . . .), color (red, blue, green), taste (sour, sweet).
    - **Comparison** is allowed when the same attributes can be matched. "Taste" may be a uniform attribute for both pears and apples and therefore a relevant comparison, while comparing a bike with an apple makes little sense as they have no attributes in common.
- Furthermore, a typical sales feature like **product bundling, configuration** and **online advisory** services can be offered if the basic product information is up to speed.
- A PIM is essential for **cross- and up-selling** which are known to increase the average purchase amount. In the ROI study conducted by Heiler, retailers with a PIM system created far more relationships between products than those without a PIM.

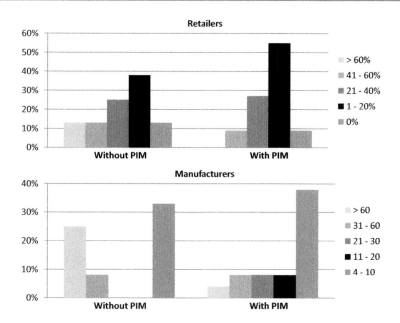

Fig. 2.4 Time needed to change the information for one product on the Web shop

- To conclude, with more and more accurate product information, the customer feels **less uncertainty** about his possible purchase.

Apart from increased conversion in the digital channel, conversion may also increase via other channels like customer care and in the sales force by enabling them with better product information. For example, The Yankee Group reports a 25 % enhancement within Customer Service due to the introduction of a PIM system.

In short, a PIM system can help revenues grow in several ways. How much depends on several factors. However, overall Aberdeen reports a growth in revenue of up to 20 % and more.

2.3.2   Less Cost (or Better Information)

PIM can reduce the cost per product in several ways:
- **Faster information retrieval**: Aberdeen measured a reduction in time searching for information of 2 working hours a week per employee. A different study shows search time is reduced by more than 25 % with the introduction of a PDM (Könst et al. 2009). Heiler's ROI study also confirms improvement in search time. Before the introduction of a PIM system, less than 17 % of staff at manufacturing companies spend less than 2 h per week searching for products. After implementation this percentage had grown to 36 %. For retailers this percentage grew from 47 % to 58 %.

- **Faster editing**: It became clear in the ROI study by Heiler that a PIM can also influence the speed at which a product can be edited. Both retailers and manufacturers with a PIM needed less time to edit a product than companies without a PIM system, as Fig. 2.4 shows. On average retailers reported, with the introduction of a PIM system, the time to update one product was reduced by 30 %. In addition, the time needed to remove a product information error from the Web shop was reduced by 75 %. The reason for this is simple. The survey shows that 68 % of those retailers using a PIM system have only one or two systems for data maintenance, while for those retailers without a PIM this figure is only 21 %.
- **Fewer returns**: better product information not only leads to more sales, it also leads to fewer product returns (up to 23 % according to Heiler). Especially in the fashion industry, where returns are on average 20 % of all orders, being able to reduce the percentage of returns makes the difference between running a profitable Web shop or not.
- **Less data cleaning**: as PIM systems allow easy interfacing with other systems. As a result less information has to be updated manually. According to Goodmasters, 25 min per SKU per year is spent on manual item data cleaning which would take only 4 min with automatic synchronization. In other words, 20 man months per 10,000 SKUs!
- **Less double work, more re-use**: with one entry per product into the PIM system, the chances that the same product is maintained twice are strongly reduced. As product information becomes more centrally available, re-use of product information increases accordingly.
- **Less re-work**: as PIM systems offer several tools to validate product data entry the number of mistakes is significantly reduced. AT Kearney estimates that 30 % of all article data from wholesale and producers has at least one mistake in it. It estimates the cost of correction to be between 60 € and 80 € per product.
- **Fewer logistical errors:** when product information gets better fewer mistakes are made in logistical processes.[2] Proctor & Gamble discovered that 3.6 % of its orders included products that were obsolete. Johnson & Johnson also discovered that inaccurate product data caused 2.5 % out of stocks with its biggest retailer Walmart. Accurate data would be able to reduce inbound logistical costs by 0.5–1.0 % and outbound logistical costs by 0.2–0.7 %. While the percentage seems low, the cost reductions are significant when financials are involved.
- **Fewer information enquiries**: according to AT Kearney, the introduction of a PIM system resulted in 27 % fewer customer calls. When product information improves, customers have to contact the company less by phone and email to get the information they want before they buy.
- **Fewer integration costs**: according to Heiler, the time needed to integrate the offering of a supplier differs strongly per company and per supplier. In the Heiler ROI study, over 50 % of manufacturers and 59 % of retailers have to manage

---

[2] Source: GoodmastersHQ.com presentation, July 2012.

11 or more integration projects per year. In this context, 26 % of retailers have over 100 data integrations to manage. The respondents' answers make it clear that the time taken to integrate supplier data has been greatly reduced by using PIM. More than 54 % of integrations are carried out within 2 weeks; only 15 % managed to achieve this prior to the introduction of PIM. 45 % were carried out within 3–4 days (with PIM 25 %) and 35 % took 1–6 months (with PIM only 21 %).

- **Letting suppliers do the work**: PIM systems allow for the easy import of external product data, either automated or manually by the supplier itself. According to AT Kearney, savings can be significant as companies invest an average of 25 min per article per year from not synchronized data. With 100,000 products this adds up to 3 full time equivalents. However, in reality, few suppliers are yet able to provide accurate product information in a readable format. As a result, this benefit is rather industry specific and depends on the willingness and professionalism of the suppliers.
- **Outsourcing of PIM processes**: while we do not recommend any company outsource all their PIM processes, some labor intensive processes, like product enrichment and translation, can much more easily be outsourced to low cost countries than before or be purchased from an external supplier.

Overall the operational benefits of a PIM system can be significant. Aberdeen sees in its research a 67 % drop in labor cost. In a similar fashion, the Yankee Group reports an increase in employee productivity of 20 %.

However, in our own case studies we do not see the cost savings being realized. While the above-mentioned cost reductions are valid, in reality the introduction of a PIM system rarely reduced operational costs. The cost savings are usually directly invested in creating better and more complete product information and/or supporting the long-tail strategy.

To summarize, PIM systems seem to be quite able to create a positive ROI fast. According to the Yankee Group, an ROI of 25 % might even be achievable within 1 year (The Yankee Group 2005).

2.4   When to Consider a PIM System

A PIM system is not a "must have" for every company. Several factors determine whether there is a need for a PIM system:
- **Lots of products and product changes**: fashion retailers in particular change their entire assortment twice or even more times per year.
- **Lots of users**: Excel is a great tool but with a few thousand products it becomes less great, especially when several people need to work on product information at the same time.
- **Product complexity**: when products have many attributes and the kind of products offered differ widely, the cost of working with Excel or standard database systems increase sharply. PIM systems allow products to be classified much more easily.

- **Data quality/compliance**: PIM has several tools to improve and maintain the quality of product information. Usually it also logs who edits and/or approves which product content and when.
- **Lots of sources/synchronizations**: the manual import of data is doable if it involves uploading a CSV file once a week. However, synchronization of data with 15 different suppliers on a daily basis can best be automated.
- **Lots of customer segments**: the more customer segments, the more different views on the complete assortment have to be maintained.
- **Lots of channels**: the more (different) channels (print, Web, mobile, etc.) the more likely different output formats and interfaces have to be supported.
- **Countries/languages**: when providing product information in 32 countries with local adaptation of content, a PIM is no longer an option but a must have.

Even companies with a limited number of products may decide to invest in a PIM system. A premium brand producer of strollers, for example, only has three different kinds of strollers. However, the strollers are sold in over 80 countries in 13 different languages, the products have more than 1,000 variants as components may differ in color, product parts change over time and may differ per country due to regulatory demands, etc. As a result, 30+ central marketing staff and local sales employees are continuously working on product information and a PIM system proved a necessity to manage the complexity.

References

Könst, J. S., la Fontaine, J. P., & Hoogeboom, M. G. R. (2009, August). *Product data management, a strategic perspective*. Geldermalsen: Maj Engineering Publishing.
The Yankee Group. (2005, January). *The cost of waiting: Building the ROI case to implement product information management now*.

The Product Data Model

3

The biggest chunk of work when introducing a PIM system is not the integration and customization of the PIM system. Most of the time is spent on filling the PIM with useful data. However, before a PIM can be filled, you need to determine which information needs to be stored and how. This is defined in a Product Data Model.

Section 3.1 gives an overview of which kind of information can be collected. Section 3.2 lists several ways in which your organization can determine its product information need. Section 3.3 and onwards discuss the key concepts of a Product Data Model. The final part of this chapter explains how you can easily set up a Product Data Model.

3.1   Kinds of Product Information

An ERP often covers the basic product information needs:

- Article ID
- Article name
- Article description
- Size dimensions
- Weight
- Price(s)

This information is often needed to support logistical and financial processes. However, the size dimensions might not be the ones of the actual product but of the product packaging. The product information from the ERP may also encompass information relevant for the purchase and merchandise department. Generally speaking, this information is not suitable for showing to the customer. This information is usually added in the PIM system.

A PIM system can be used to enrich products for commercial purposes across three dimensions: content, commercial, and communal.

J. Abraham, *Product Information Management*, Management for Professionals,
DOI 10.1007/978-3-319-04885-7_3, © Springer International Publishing Switzerland 2014

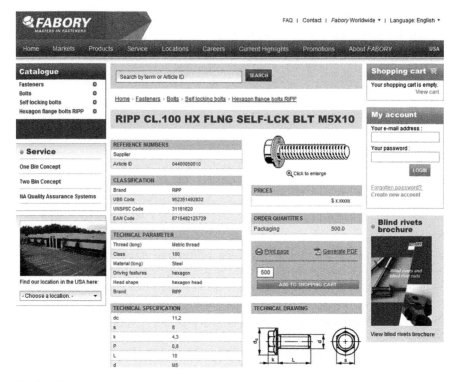

Fig. 3.1 Even something as simple as a bolt can require a large set of attributes (*Source*: Fabory. com)

3.1.1   Content Information

Content information serves to inform customers about the product. Much information can be re-used from the ERP system but information often has to be reviewed and adapted for commercial use. Typical data to be added include product attributes not required for logistical and financial processes but needed by the customer to find, compare and buy the product. Examples include the number of springs in a mattress, the number of pages in a book, etc.

The content information generally very factual. It is "need to know" information. This information category is often underestimated. Customers increasingly want more information to make a purchase decision as the example of Fabory for a simple bolt shows (see Fig. 3.1).

3.1.2   Commercial Information

Commercial information serves to inspire and entice customers to the product. All information which may help to sell the product, such as a commercial product

Fig. 3.2 An example of a product set on Leballon.nl

description, questions and answers, a high resolution product photo (or several), a listing of the key buying reasons, quality certificates, etc. Newest trends in this domain are product videos and the presentation of complete product sets as shown in Fig. 3.2.

3.1.3 Community Information

Community information serves to engage and involve customers more with the product. Information is gathered from the customers who actually use the products:

- **Product reviews** by customers who have bought the products. E.g. Ebags.com believes reviews are nearly as important as basic information and maybe even more so, see also Fig. 3.3;
- **Photos** of the product as actually used by the consumer. E.g. at Mammut.ch;
- **Statistical data** about how often the products were viewed and bought. E.g. Bookings.com tells you how many consumers are looking at the same hotel as you at the same time;
- **Facebook likes and profiles** e.g. TheSting.nl shows the profiles of people who have bought the product before and if they include your friends. Of course with the user's permission.

Fig. 3.3 eBags.com combines rich video content with product reviews

All this information can help convince other customers to buy the product.

The latest development in this domain is that customers can answer questions from others online in a kind of forum, and add their own tags to products to describe it better and allow other customers to find the product more easily.

3.2   How to Determine Your Information Need

There are several methods to determine what information you need to collect and store, including:

- **Asking the editors**: these people might be working at different departments within your organization, like sales and marketing. Purchasing and logistics may also have wishes that are not currently supported by the ERP system used. Analyzing the current information they store on paper, in Excel sheets and other systems can give you a good start.
- **Asking end-users**: we already defined the possible different channels in Sect. 1.5.2. Each of these channels has end-users. Asking them what information they need is a simple step. However, end-users rarely know what they want and it is

difficult for them to give a complete picture. End-users usually tend to underestimate or over-exaggerate their information need.

- **"Steal" from competitors**: the expression "better to copy a good idea than come up with a bad one yourself" certainly applies to PIM. Viewing competitors' print catalogs and Web shops to create your own base for a product data model (and of course improve on it) may not be chic but it helps make a kick-start.
- **Use existing product information models**: models of categories and attributes already exist for several industries. Section 4.3.3 discusses a number of them. If they apply to your industry it is wise to start here instead of creating a proprietary model which may make importing data cumbersome and may not be accepted by your channels.

In the end it is crucial that the entire information need of all users of the information is covered. A common mistake is to look mainly at the sales processes. However, the entire customer journey has to be supported which also means the part in which the product is used for the first time, when replacement parts have to be bought, and how the product is disposed of.

3.3 Key PIM Concepts

In Sect. 1.3.3 we briefly discussed categorization and classification as a way to organize products and their attributes. In this section we will dive a lot deeper into these core PIM concepts.

3.3.1 Catalogs

A catalog is in essence nothing more than a collection of products. Catalogs can best be compared to assortments. A company may offer different catalogs:

- one for its vegetable buyers;
- one for its fruit buyers;
- one for buyers who buy both vegetables and fruit;
- and personalized catalogs for big customers with a collection of vegetables and/or fruit.

There may even be temporary catalogs for projects. CRH, a construction material selling company, for example, has a B2B Web site where customers can login, choose a specific construction project, and order those specific bricks, plaster and other materials, specified previously during the purchase process (see the CRH case).

3.3.2   Product Categories

Categories can be used to sort the products within a catalog into smaller sub-sections. Within the catalog for fruit you could, for example, create the following categories:
- Local fruit
- Exotic fruit

Each of these categories (also called main or super-categories) can have sub-categories and sub-sub-categories, etc. An example:
- Local fruit:
  - Apples
    Elstar
    Golden Delicious
    Jonagold
  - Pears
    Conference
    Doyenne
    Durondeau
- Exotic fruit
  - Kiwi
    Golden Kiwi
    Mini Kiwi
  - Pineapple

The structure above is referred to as a category tree (alternative names are product trees or product taxonomies).

The same product can be part of multiple category trees. For customers the sorting used above may be logical but the procurement department may prefer a categorization more like this:
- Supplier A
  - Elstar
  - Golden Delicious
  - Durondeau
- Supplier B
  - Elstar
  - Conference
  - Mini Kiwi
- Supplier C
  - Pineapple

Likewise the financial department may again prefer a different way of organizing products:
- Margin group A (10 %)
  - Elstar
  - Golden Delicious
  - Durondeau
  - ...

- Margin group B (20 %)
  - Golden Kiwi
  - Mini Kiwi
  - Pineapple
- Tax group 6 %
  - Elstar
  - Golden Delicious
  - Durondeau
  - ...
- Tax group 19 %
  - Golden Kiwi
  - Mini Kiwi
  - Pineapple

Entirely different category structures can also be set up for channels. A structure based on product popularity may be logical for a Web site, whereas products in alphabetical order may be preferable for a print catalog.

Likewise, categories may differ for countries, customer segments, etc. For example, in Hawaii the ordering of products may be as follows:

- Local fruit
  - Kiwi
  - Pineapple
- Exotic fruit
  - Apples
  - Pears

It is all in the eye of the beholder.

3.3.3   Product Categorization Rules

Different rules may apply when you set up a category:

- **Products in nodes and/or leaves**: a node has sub-categories while a leaf (of a category tree) has no subcategories. Some category systems only allow products to be sorted into the leaf position of a category tree while others also allow products to be put into nodes.
- **Structured versus unstructured trees**: depending on the goal of the category structures, a product may only be placed in one node or leaf or in several. For example, do not ask me why, but Kiwis are officially no longer an exotic fruit on the Dutch market. However, most consumers do not know this. A category manager may therefore decide to place Kiwis in both categories.

Most ERP systems allow only one kind of category structure, usually with products only in the leaves and with one product only allowed at one place within the category structure (thus a structured tree). This structure is often called the master category tree.

The master category tree is usually the base tree for the PIM system on which basis more channel and user-oriented structures can be created.

3.3.4   Product Classification Classes

Classification classes (abbreviated: CC) are to some extent very similar to categories. A hierarchy of classification classes can be created, also called a schema or taxonomy. However, a classification class does not contain products but product attributes.

- CC-Fruit:
    - Name
    - Product ID
    - Product description
    - Taste
    - Weight
    - Kind
    - CC-Local
      Producer
    - CC-Exotic
      Country
      Wholesaler

In the example above you see that the classification class "Fruit" contains six main product attributes: "Name", "ProductID", "Product description", "Taste", "Weight" and "Kind". The classification class "Fruit" also contains two sub-classification classes, namely "Local" and "Exotic". The sub-classification class "Local" has one kind of attribute called "Producer". The sub-classification class "Exotic" has two kinds of attributes.

The reason for this distinction is that our fruit trader for Local fruits wants to know the name of the producer. For Exotic fruits this information is either not relevant or not known. However, the country of origin and wholesaler is relevant.

Products and product categories can now be assigned to these classification classes. This results in the example above in all products in the category "Local Fruit" to have the attributes "Taste", "Weight", "Kind" and "Producer". Products in the "Exotic Fruit" category have the same generic attributes. However, Exotic Fruit does not have the attribute "Producer" but instead has "Country" and "Wholesaler" as additional attributes.

Why do classification classes exist? Classification allows the product attributes to be sorted into collections. This has several advantages:

- **Keeping it manageable**: in our example we only have six attributes. Most companies however have thousands of different kinds of products and each kind of product might have several unique attributes. If attributes were not sorted into collections, users would continuously be confronted with a list of thousands of attributes. In this way attributes can be found easily, added, removed and their properties changed.
- **Only show relevant attributes**: sorting attributes into collections and assigning them to specific product categories, allows the PIM system to only show relevant attributes. If data is entered for Local Fruit, the attributes "Country" and "Wholesaler" do not apply and are therefore not shown. Likewise, for example,

on a Web site, if a visitor wants to sort Exotic Fruit by Country, he can, but when he is looking at Local Fruit, he cannot, as it is not a relevant attribute.

3.3.5   Features, Attributes and Values

Product attributes are nothing more than **properties of a product**. Separating attributes as a concept of the product itself allows the attribute to be re-used for multiple products and product categories. This for example allows a user to compare different kinds of fruit on the attribute "Taste".

Some attributes apply to all the products in the assortment. Each product for example has a "Unique Product Identifier", "Name" and "Product description". These attributes are often distinguished from attributes that only apply to part of the collection of products. Some PIM suppliers call these "**Features**". Others do not make the distinction.

We already explained that Attributes are assigned to Classification Classes. Similarly, values can be assigned to Attributes. There are several kinds of **Values** that can be linked to an attribute. The most common are:

- **Boolean**: the value is either "Yes" or "No".
- **String**: a line of text. The product name for example is usually a string.
- **Text**: a large text field, which in some PIM systems can be media rich (e.g. support different types of fonts, colors, sizes and features like making text bold, underlined, etc.). Typically the "Product description" is a text field.
- **Number**: a number like 1.7, -10, 3.145, etc.
- **List**: for a product only a value can be selected that is part of a predefined list.
  - **Single value**: only one value can be selected. An apple for example is usually either Red, Yellow or Green.
  - **Multi value**: more than one value can be selected. A dress may have multiple colors for example Red and Green.

Most PIM systems support more kinds of attributes or even allow users to define their own kinds of attributes.

Going back to our Fruit example, the classification class model is expanded with values:

- CC-Fruit:
  - Name (String)
  - Product ID (Number/Integer)
  - Product description (Text)
  - Taste (Single value List with the values "Sweet", "Sour", "Undefined".
  - Weight (Number/Integer)
  - Kind (Single value List with the values "Apple", "Pear", "Kiwi" and "Pineapple")
  - CC-Local
    Producer (Single value List with the values "John Fruit Producers", "The Basket Company")
  - CC-Exotic

Country (Single value List with the values "New Zealand", "Hawaii").

Wholesaler (Single value List with the values "Fruit Import/Export Company" and "Hawaiian Fruits & Co.")

As you can see, determining which attributes and values to add is an important task. The value "Undefined" allows product specialists to choose this value, while we know that each fruit in the end has a taste. Allowing data entry staff to choose the value "Undefined" is dangerous for the quality of the product data. In my experience data entry staff are usually under considerable pressure to add data. Choosing the easy way out if the information is not immediately known is quickly done, possibly resulting in dozens of fruits with as Taste "Undefined".

The taste however might be difficult to describe in being only "Sweet" or "Sour". One of the benefits of a PIM system is that the administrator can quickly add values to attributes. Changing Taste from a single to a multi value list allows product specialists to also enter combinations of taste. Alternatively a value could be added "Sweet/Sour".

Likewise the PIM administrator may want to make some additional changes. Hawaii for example is not formally a country. However, from a commercial point of view, it may not be wise to state that the county of origin is the "United States of America" as it sounds a lot less "Exotic". For legal and logistical reasons, an additional attribute could be added called "Formal country" with values like "the Netherlands" and "United States of America". Or the attribute "Country" could be renamed "Region".

As you can see determining the names of attributes and their values is not something done easily nor at one go. It is usually a continuous process of smaller and larger improvements.

3.3.6 Units

Most PIM systems allow for the automatic conversion of metric systems. For example, the 1.5 L contents of a Coca Cola bottle can be stored in a PIM system in several ways:

- As part of a product description: "Contains 1.5 L"
- As part of an attribute named "Content" with value "1.5 L"
- As part of an attribute named "Content" with value "1.5" and unit "L"

The last example allows you to make metric conversions and is usually the best way to go. E.g. the value 1.5 can be converted to 0.4 US gallons and 2.6 imperial pints as we know that the value of the unit was measured in Ls.

Working with units allows data (temperature, mass, length, time, etc.) to be entered once and be recalculated for countries where a different metric system applies. This avoids double entries and conversion errors.

Units can also be used for handy conversions. For example, customers can be advised on how much of a material they need to accomplish a certain task with the product:

- 1 L of paint covers 4 m^2 of a wall

- 1 package of 5 planks of laminate allows you to lay a floor of 7 m^2
  Or to stick with our Fruit example: 10 apples are needed to make one apple cake.

3.3.7 Digital Assets

Most PIM systems have the option to store digital assets and connect them to other concepts within the PIM system, such as Categories and Products but in some PIM systems also Attributes and even Values.

Digital assets can be any kind of BLOB (Binary Large Object). Examples include photos, CAD/CAM documents, PDF files, videos, etc. A digital asset can usually be connected to multiple categories and products at the same time.

3.3.8 Products, Variants, Articles and SKUs

So far we have used the term "Product" to describe physical goods and services sold to customers. Within PIM systems "Products", also called "Base Products" or "Base Units/Items" are often a virtual presentation of a physical good, the "Variants".

Variants are the actual Stock Keeping Units (SKUs), also called articles or items. Variants exist physically and have a price and stock level. Products are a higher level conceptualization of Variants. An example:

Coca Cola offers its Coca Cola drink in several containers:
- 0.5 L Coca Cola bottle
- 1.0 L Coca Cola bottle
- 1.5 L Coca Cola bottle

The contents of all these three bottles is exactly the same. The bottle is also made from the same material. The bottles just differ in size. The following information needs to be stored for each container:
- Article ID: A unique identifier that differs per container.
- Product name: this could, in theory, be the same for all three containers, namely "Coca Cola". In practice it may be wise to add the size of the bottle to differentiate.
- Product description: a marketing text, the same for all three containers.
- Ingredients: a technical description of the soft drink.
- Volume: in our case, three different values can apply: 0.5 L, 1.0 L and 1.5 L (where we of course distinguish between the unit "L" and its values "0.5", "1.0" and "1.5").

The same information can be entered three times. However, this implies a lot of double (actually triple) work. And if, for example, the product description or ingredients change, the information has to be updated three times. This is not only extra work but also error prone and does not fit the idea of having a PIM system where all information is stored only once.

A better solution would be to create a product hierarchy where there is one product, with three variants.

- Coca Cola Bottle:
  - 0.5 L
  - 1.0 L
  - 1.5 L

Information is then stored on two different levels. On the product level the data for "Product description" and "Ingredients" is stored. On the variant level the "Article ID", "Product Name" and "Volume" are stored. In short, all attribute values that are shared, should be maintained on the product level. Those values that differ are stored on the variant level.

Again, the administrator of the PIM may decide to move the "Product Name" to the product level. Commercially you may want to name the product "1.0 L Coca Cola bottle" However, this can also be done by first showing the value "1.0", then the unit name "L" followed by the product name "Coca Cola bottle". The administrator may even decide to create a separate attribute called "Container" with value "bottle".

Of course the above example is rather simple. However, if you have a T-shirt in five sizes and eight colors, making a distinction between the product and its variants becomes much more interesting for several reasons:

- **Efficiency**: No data has to be maintained double.
- **Presentation**: Showing the same T-shirt 40 times in an online search result may just irritate or confuse the customer. It is better to allow him or her first to find the right product and then select the right variant.

There are no golden rules for how to group different SKUs into a product and its variants. Typical attributes that are maintained on the variant level are:

- Color (red, blue, yellow)
- Size (S, M, L, XL)
- Packaging kind (package, box, container)

However, here are a few tips:

- All variants below a product should always be exactly the same apart from one or two attributes on which they differ.
- Think from the customer's point of view when grouping SKUs into products. A customer may consider a 0.5 L Coca Cola product to be really different from a 1.5 L Coca Cola product. However, he probably considers a white T-shirt in five sizes to be the same. A simple trick to determine if an attribute should be "variant defining" is to imagine the following two situations:
  - Would it be more logical from a customer's point of view to see all products on a product lister page on a Web shop? If so, then the attribute should not be a variant defining attribute.
  - Would it be more logical from a customer's point of view to see the attribute as a choice (a dropdown box in our example) on the product detail page of a Web site. If so, then the attribute should be a variant defining attribute.
- In general we recommend keeping the number of attributes that make a variant differ from others low, e.g. 1 or 2. More are, of course, possible but it becomes

Fig. 3.4 On Bugaboo.com five attributes determine the actual variant

increasingly more difficult for a customer to understand which choices he can make (see Fig. 3.4).

In the remaining chapters we will use the term "product" where it may often also be applicable for variants, SKUs or items.

3.4   Combining the PIM Concepts

So far we have discussed several key concepts of a PIM system individually. However, their strengths lie in combining them. Figure 3.5 shows how the different concepts interact.

A classification class can be related to several attributes and these attributes can (if they are a list) have multiple values. When category and classification classes are linked, all the products within that category also inherit the attributes of the classification class.

In theory, a classification class can be linked to all kinds of categories and even to individual products. In practice the data is often structured according to the set-up as shown in Fig. 3.6. In the PIM system a master catalog is set up where each product only exists once (this is often a copy of the way the products are ordered in the ERP system). Next, the categories within the master catalog are linked to the

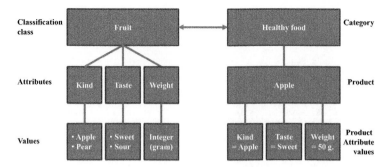

Fig. 3.5 A category inherits attributes from a classification class

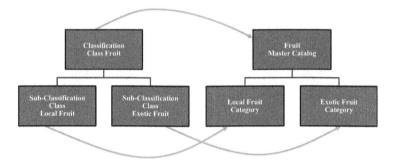

Fig. 3.6 Linking a classification tree to a master product category tree

classification classes. In this way the products can be given the right attributes quickly.

3.5   Creating a Product Data Model

Creating a product data model can be a laborious task. The more different kinds of products, the more work has to be done before you can actually start entering data. The challenge is that creating an efficient and well set-up product data model requires considerable data modeling expertise. However, it also requires industry and product knowledge. Both expertises are rarely combined in one person.

We therefore recommend customers adopt the following (simplified) approach:

3.5.1   Determine the Internal Master Product Category Tree

First determine all relevant product categories and organize them in an intuitive tree. Product categories may already have been defined in the ERP system. These can serve as the basis. What is important is that the product categories are **intuitive**

for the internal user. What is also important is that the tree structure should be unique; product categories should not overlap and one product should be placed in one product category leaf only.

Let's take a new example based one of our cases: Beter Bed:

- Box springs and bedsteads:
  - Box springs
  - Bedsteads
    Grown-up bedsteads
    Children's bedsteads
  - Sleep sofas
- Mattresses
  - Pocket Suspension
  - Latex
  - Memory Foam
  - Polyether

3.5.2   List All Attributes Per Category

The next step is to list all the relevant attributes for the lowest level of categories (the leaves of the product category tree). We already know that some attributes apply to all the products in the assortment (product ID, description, size dimensions, etc.). These can be written down at the top. However, the remaining attributes should all be written down per category.

- Generic features
  - Product ID
  - Product description
  - Height
  - Width
  - Length
- Box springs and bedsteads:
  - Box springs
    Brand
    Material box spring
    Weight class
    Comfort zones
- Bedsteads
  - Grown-up bedsteads
    Brand
    Material bedsteads
  - Children's bedsteads
    Brand
    Material bedsteads
    Suitable for
- Mattresses

– Pocket Suspension

. . .

While creating the list of attributes, please consider the tips given in Sect. 3.2.

3.5.3 Transform to a Classification Structure

The next step is to transform the category tree and attributes to a classification tree. This is done by moving double attributes one "trunk" up one level, until they are unique.
- Generic features
  - Product ID
  - Product description
  - Height
  - Width
  - Length
  - **Brand**
- Box springs and bedsteads:
  - Box springs
    Brand
    Material box spring
    Weight class
    Comfort zones
- Bedsteads
  - **Material bedsteads**
    - Grown-up bedsteads
      Brand
      Material bedsteads
    - Children's bedsteads
      Brand
      Material bedsteads
      Suitable for
- Mattresses
  - Pocket Suspension

    . . .

In our example, the attribute "Brand" is moved to the list of generic features as it is an attribute for all product categories. Material bedsteads is moved up one level. One could argue that changing the name of "Material box spring" and "Material bedsteads" to "Material" would result in the same attribute. However the materials used for box springs and bedsteads is entirely different and this customer has therefore chosen to keep them separate to prevent confusion. Finally, the category "Grown-up bedsteads" can be removed as there are no longer any attributes in it.

3.5.4 Enrich Each Attribute

Each attribute has to be enriched to improve the quality of the product data. Some examples:

- **Attribute description**: it might be helpful to briefly describe what the attribute is about. Some attributes in the example above might seem to be self-explanatory but for an outsider even the term "Brand" can be confusing. The attribute description can also be part of the data which is distributed to the different channels as an explanatory description.
- **Attribute type:** e.g. Boolean, Text, Number, etc. We already described these in Sect. 3.3.5.
- **Unit type:** if the attribute type is a number, a unit type may be applicable such as "kilo", "cm", etc. Make sure to be uniform in the definition of your unit types (e.g. "cm." or "cm" but not both).
- **List values**: if the attribute type is a list, then they also need to be defined.
- **Mandatory**: is filling in the attribute mandatory or not.
- **Restrictions**: restrictions might be applicable to the value entered for the attribute, such as:
  - Has a minimum value
  - Has a maximum value
  - Number of decimals
  - etc.
- **Base of variant**: does the attribute have the same value for all products or not? In other words, does the attribute define the variants of a product as color and size often do for clothing. See Sect. 3.3.8.
- **Source system**: which system will fill in the values of this attribute for the first time. This is likely to be the ERP system or a different external source as defined in Sect. 1.5.1 if it concerns attributes such as price and stock. For other attributes the ERP system may be used to fill the fields once. From that point onwards the PIM is usually the master system.
- **Master system**: as already stated for source systems, the source system may only be used once after which the PIM system becomes the lead system (also called master). For price and stock information, external source systems usually remain the master system.

In addition, attribute enrichment can be done for channel-specific needs, e.g. as for a Web site:

- **Show as variant defining attribute**: even if an attribute defines the variants of a product, there may be reasons not to show it on the product detail page as such, as the number of choices becomes too large or customers prefer to make the choice for the specific attribute earlier in the process (e.g. on the product lister page).
- **Free text search**: should the values of the attribute be searched is the user users free text search to search through the assortment or should these values be ignored?
- **Filter search**: should the attribute be used as a filter on the product lister page?

- **Access rules**: which user groups (internal, external) can view/edit the attribute value?
- **Show if empty**: should the variable be shown if it has no value?
- **Show for comparison**: should the attribute be shown on a comparison page?
- **Order**: in which order should the attribute be shown in relation to other attributes in the same classification class and across all classification classes?
- etc.

Likewise, attribute specific enrichments (i.e. should it be shown or not) can be done for other channels like print, mobile, etc.

3.6   Maintaining the Product Data Model

A product data model is never finished. New product categories are added and removed over time. Feedback and insights will also result in new attributes being added while rarely used ones might be archived.

There are several ways to get continuous feedback:

- **Click path analysis**: how do customers navigate your channels? Can they find the product they are looking for immediately or are their paths rather chaotic, which may be a sign that the product category tree is not customer oriented.
- **Keyword analysis**: which words are used to search for products. It might be the case that attributes are used to limit search results. In the case of Beter Bed, "anti allergic mattress" indicated that customers want to know if a mattress is anti allergic or not.
- **Category conversion analysis**: analyzing the purchase to category visit ratio may lead to insights. It may be that the prices of the products in the category are too high but often the product information itself is too limited to make the sale.

In short, improving your Product Data Model should never be a one-off activity.

PIM Processes

4

Over the past 10 years Unic has developed a requirements gathering methodology called "The Process Landscapes" (see Fig. 4.1). In this methodology Unic employees have written down all the e-commerce and PIM processes the company has automated at one time or another. For each of these main processes Unic also defined the sub-processes, and for these again the sub-sub-processes (or items), and on the lowest level the user stories. A user story is a short description in everyday language that captures what a user wants to do with the system on such a detailed level that the developer can program this.

In this chapter we discuss all the major PIM processes and their sub-processes. We do not go so far as to list all user stories, although we do realize that this may be quite handy for making a request for proposal. However, as PIM systems are continuously developing, so are the underlying user stories. Paper is therefore not the best medium.

In order to limit tedious explanations, we use the term "management" and "maintenance" of items often in this chapter. Management includes standard features such as searching, filtering, creating, editing and archiving items of, among others, products, variants, categories, etc.

4.1 Master Data Management

The first PIM process is called Master Data Management. Master Data defines the core information of the products. Typical master data include its creation date, the product identification number, stock level(s), prices, delivery times, etc. It is, in essence, the data required for logistical and commercial purposes. In most cases, that kind of data is generated by ERP systems. This may also involve data from suppliers. Master data are the foundation of the entire data structure.

From this basic data management process, a division is made into the various sub-processes.

J. Abraham, *Product Information Management*, Management for Professionals,
DOI 10.1007/978-3-319-04885-7_4, © Springer International Publishing Switzerland 2014

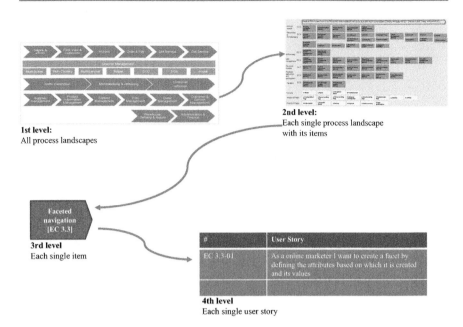

1st level:
All process landscapes

2nd level:
Each single process landscape
with its items

**Faceted
navigation
[EC 3.3]**

3rd level
Each single item

#	User Story
EC 3.3-01	As a online marketer I want to create a facet by defining the attributes based on which it is created and its values

4th level
Each single user story

Fig. 4.1 Unic's process landscape model

4.1.1   Importing Master Data

Importing Master data from sources into the PIM system sounds trivial but it includes several steps such as validating whether the product already exists and if not, creating the product in the PIM system for the first time and then enriching the product with the master data from the sources. It is not only the company's own sources that can generate data, it can also be generated by suppliers or originate from external data libraries.

4.1.2   Synchronization

The core part of this process is the modification of master data within the PIM system via synchronization with the source systems. It is crucial that this process is clearly defined in the Product Data Model. Which fields are only imported once and from then onwards maintained in the PIM system? Which fields are continuously synchronized from the source systems, e.g. where the source systems remain the master (see Sect. 3.5.4)?

4.1.3   Supplier Consolidation

One and the same product can be delivered by several suppliers. However, only one product should be presented to the customer. Product information from different suppliers has therefore to be consolidated into one set of data. This becomes particularly handy when, for example, one supplier has a good product description, the other more detailed technical attribute information, and a third delivers the best product photos. The PIM system then has to determine, on a product by product basis, which information from which supplier it imports and uses in its PIM system. Several PIM systems allow administrators to immediately define business rules for importing data without programming skills.

4.1.4   Competitor Consolidation

Product information from competing companies can also be managed in PIM. This can be a desired feature in several ways. A crawler or scraper function is used to download information from the Web and add it to the PIM system.

The feature can be used to compare assortments to determine which products the competitor offers and the company does not and vice versa. The process also allows for price comparison, which is a very powerful feature if you follow a price strategy, as Fokkido does (see Fig. 4.2). Importing prices from competitors might even allow for automatic price adaptation of your own products.

A more disputable application is that it can also be used to enrich one's own products with product information from competitors, which is, in fact, nothing other than theft. According to the law in most countries, the copying of (product) information from other Web sites and presenting it as your own is a criminal offence.

4.1.5   Brand Management

Products have a manufacturer (the one who produces the product), suppliers (the companies that supply the product) and a brand (the type name under which this product is sold). The lists of these different names (combined "Brand") need to be maintained.

Also here **import** and **synchronization** of data is often needed as companies may work with several thousand manufacturers, suppliers and related brands.

In addition, the names of these products are rarely directly re-usable as the source systems have often maintained brands in a non-customer representative way. Typically the following errors are found:

- HOB-S-12: Codes are used instead of real brand names. In this case HOB12 stands for House of Benetton 2012 Summer Collection.

Fig. 4.2 Price comparison at Fokkido.nl

- 8mm/8MILLIMETER: Different names are used for the same brand name. It may seem a minor error but it looks amateurish when shown across your channels (see Fig. 4.3).
- No Brand: The product does not have a brand name. This may be fine, however it may then be better not to show a brand name instead of "NULL" (a database term which means no value has been defined) or use a household (fake) brand name.

To remove these kinds of errors they can either be fixed in the source system or in the PIM system. Of course, fixing errors in the source system in the best way. Indeed, it is the responsibility of the source system to deliver clean data. In practice it may just be faster and politically more realistic to clean the data up in the PIM system, especially when source data comes from systems outside the organization. Therefore most PIM systems offer **mapping** functionality to transform brand names used by the source to represent product information in the PIM system.

In addition, **brands can be enriched** in the PIM system to include visuals, logos, contact details, descriptions, reviews, etc. These can be re-used if pages about the brand are created, either for print, online or other channels.

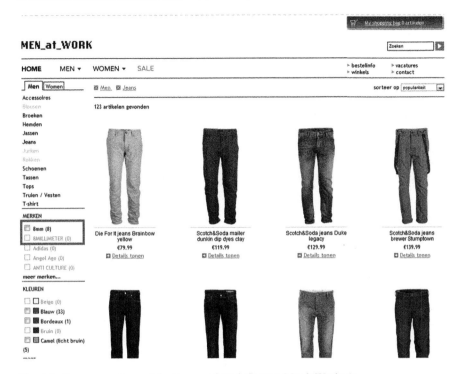

Fig. 4.3 Two names are used for the same brand (Source: MenAtWork.nl)

4.1.6 Management of Composition Products

Often companies do not only sell individual products but also products composed of several other products. There are several kinds:

- **Bundles**: bundles are typical marketing creations. A bundle combines several products together under a separate product ID. Usually a different (discount) price also applies. The products can, however, usually also be bought individually. In fashion, for example, bundles are becoming more popular as Fig. 3.2 shows. But also at Nikon bundles of, for example, a camera, bag and extra flash disc, are often created on both international as well as local level for promotion purposes (see the Nikon Europe case in Sect. 8.7).
- **Sets**: a set consists of several sub-parts that are not individually available for purchase. Sets are usually created because the individual parts do not have any value. At Beter Bed Holding, for example, bedsteads are sold with special bedstead legs if a customer buys a bedstead together with an electric bed frame (the electric motor requires a slightly higher bed and therefore higher feet). The feet are part of the product but have a separate article ID because they have to be picked separately in the warehouse. The products can however not be bought separately (see the Beter Bed Holding case in Sect. 8.1).

- **Composites**: a composite consists of several sub-parts that are sellable themselves. Often these products stick in the middle. It is logical to buy them as a whole but it also happens that individual items are bought stand alone. A typical example is a garden table set. Customers usually buy a set of four chairs with a table, but sometimes the table or chairs are bought individually.

All these kinds of products have to be managed. Again, it may start with **importing and synchronization** of data when composite products already exist in the source systems. This is often the case for sets. However, bundles often have to be created and maintained in the PIM system. Typical features are not only the **bundle creation** but also managing when a bundle becomes active, at which price, and when the bundle is dissolved again.

4.1.7 Product Variant Creation

Most ERP systems do not differentiate between products and variants as PIM systems do. In Sect. 3.3.8 we explained the benefits of creating a virtual product with underlying "real" variants. A PIM system has to support the **creation of products** and **assignment of variants** to these products. Doing this manually is nice for handling exceptions, but the number of variants is usually too large to do this manually for each SKU.

Therefore PIM systems have to support the **automatic assignment** of SKUs to products. This is usually based on the master data it imports. A clean example is where the ERP system already used a well-structured product ID set to group related variants. In the example below, for example, the first 6 digits are unique to the product, while the second one determines the variant. The PIM system can use this data to create one product with three variants.

SKUs in the ERP system	Product and variants in the PIM system
123456-001	• 123456 (Product)
123456-002	○ 123456-001 (Variant)
123456-003	○ 123456-002 (Variant)
	○ 123456-003 (Variant)

Unfortunately most source systems have a less structured product data model and more complex business rules are needed. In essence, all master data that is imported can be used to create products and assign variants.

An example of a more complex business rule:
- If the category name in the ERP system is the same;
- And if the supplier name is the same;
- And if the name of the first part of the product name is the same;
- Then combine the SKUs into one product and underlying variants.

However, there are several situations where SKUs can only be mapped manually to products, which is a very laborious task if it entails more than 100,000 SKUs.

4.2   Category Management

4.2.1   Category Import, Synchronization and Mapping

We discussed the concept of Categories in Sect. 3.3.2. As is the case for Master Data, categories can also be **imported** from and **synchronized** with source systems. The category tree used in the ERP system can often be re-used one-on-one in the PIM system as Master Category Tree.

As is the case for master data, **mapping** is often needed as categories cannot be used one-on-one towards customers as ERP category names are not intuitive and their structure is often based on the internal structure of the company.

4.2.2   Category Enrichment

Like brands, categories can be enriched. **Typical enrichments** are:
- Category descriptions;
- Photo and video material;
- Access rules (which user groups may view and/or edit the products within the category).

As for product attributes, channel-specific category attributes can be added, such as:
- Keywords and meta tags that can be used for search engine optimization online;
- Color codes, font styles that can be used for creating a print catalog;
- Etc.

4.2.3   Category Tree Management

In Sect. 3.3.2 we explained that there may be a need for multiple category trees. **Maintaining** these category structures is less easy than often thought. For example, deleting a main category also implies the removal of lower level categories in the same branch. However, administrators may want to "tie" these categories to different branches or gain insight into products that are no longer represented in the category tree. Therefore **control** processes become important in order to prevent products from not being assigned to a category or product being assigned double where this is not desired.

4.2.4   Category Product Assignment

Products may not only need to be assigned to a Master Category but also to one or more other kinds of category trees. This can be done in several ways:

By **mapping** master categories to channel categories, channel categories can quickly be filled with products. The PIM system is, in effect, told to "place" all products within a master category also in another category.

A more refined way of assigning products to categories is based on **rules**. E.g. all products with a discount or all products with showroom models can be placed in a special category to help customers find the right product. Even entire category structures can be created based on rules. By tagging products as being meant for a special event like "Christmas", "Valentine" or "Easter" it is possible to quickly set up filtered product category trees with only the relevant products.

Of course mapping is rather crude. Master categories are set up for internal use while channel categories are meant for external use. Likewise, filling categories based on rules requires products to be enriched to allow filtering to take time. PIM systems therefore also allow the **manual placement** and removal of individual products from categories.

4.2.5   Product Ranking, Sort Order Definition

A final category management process that has to be supported is product ranking and sorting. The organization might prefer to place some products higher within a category because their margins are higher or there is too much inventory. Products can be **ranked manually** by giving them a higher priority but also based on **business rules** (e.g. show first the product with the largest difference between sales price and purchase price).

Customers on the Internet are used to defining the way products are sorted to a large extent themselves and best practice seems to be to sort on lowest price first. In print catalogs sorting on ID or name is a logical way of doing this. Still, in some instances the company may want to first show products in their own way e.g. the newest or the most popular.

4.3   Classification and Attribute Management

4.3.1   Classification Management

We discussed classifications in Sect. 3.3.4. The classification management processes support the creation and **maintenance** of **classification classes, classification trees** and **attributes**. Likewise, it supports in **assigning attributes to classification classes**. Assignment is more extensive as classification classes and attributes can be linked to several other classification classes. Like categories, classification classes and attributes can be **enriched** with descriptions, visuals, access rules, etc.

4.3.2 Attribute Management

Section 3.3.5 looked at the concept of attributes and the different elements of an attribute that can be maintained. One enrichment may require further explanation: **sorting**.

In addition, as with products within a category, attributes may also be ordered depending on a channel. Two kinds of sorting are supported:

- **Within a classification class**: e.g. within the classification class Exotic Fruit we may first want to show the attribute "Kind" and then "Country".
- **Across classification classes**: we may first want to show "Taste" and then "Kind" and "Country", followed by "Weight".

The sorting might be applicable for all channels or a specific channel. An example:

For pears we want to show on the Web the attributes of pears in the following order:

- Product name
- Price
- Weight

For apples however the order is different (e.g. because it is more natural from a customer perspective):

- Product name
- Weight
- Price

Another typical PIM functionality is which attributes are shown across which channels and how the channel should behave if no value is known for an attribute (e.g. show it or not).

4.3.3 Standard Classification Systems

There are several standard or industry classification systems that organize products into predefined category trees. Some examples are[1]:

- **Central Product Classification (CPC)**: is a product classification for goods and services promoted by the United Nations Statistical Commission. It is intended to be an international standard for organizing and analyzing data on industrial production, national accounts, trade, prices, etc.
- **Classification of Products by Activity (CPA)**: is the classification of products (goods and services) by the European Union. They provide the basis for collecting and calculating statistics on production, distributive trade, consumption, foreign trade and transport of products.

---

[1] Source: http://en.wikipedia.org/wiki/Product_classification and http://faculty.philau.edu/russowl/product.html

- **eClass**: also written as eCl@ss, is a product classification and description standard for information exchange between customers and their suppliers. eCl@ss is a de facto standard in the German energy industry and competes with UNSPSC. In 2006 eCl@ss joined forces with ETIM, which is an important standard in the wholesale electrical industry. Mid February 2011 release 7.0 of eCl@ss was published introducing substantial increase of content and being harmonized with the industry standards ETIM and Prolist (for products in the process control and chemical industry).
- **Electro-Technical Information Model (ETIM)**: is an initiative to standardize the electronic exchange of product data for electrical and electronic products (electrical installation products, home appliances and consumer electronics) to enable the electronic trading of these products. ETIM is commonly used in the creation of product catalogs. The transfer of catalog data is in an expanded BMEcat format. Since 1 January 2006 ETIM has been a member of eCl@ss and vice versa.
- **Global Product Classification (GPC)**: is defined by GS1, formally called EAN International. GS1 is an international not-for-profit association that develops standards to improve the efficiency of supply and demand chains globally and across multiple sectors. GPC is the basis for the Global Data Synchronization Network (GDSN). The Global Data Synchronization Network (GDSN) is an Internet-based network that enables companies around the globe to exchange standardized and synchronized supply chain data with their trading partners using the GPC standard. All currently published GPC content is available free of charge, without any usage restrictions. The GPC is being aligned with UNSPCS.
- **Harmonized Commodity Description and Coding System or Harmonized System (HS)**: is an internationally standardized system of names and numbers for classifying traded products. HS is developed and maintained by the World Customs Organization (WCO). As more than 206 countries apply the system, representing 96 % of all world trade, it is especially handy for global wholesalers and distributors as each country bases its own custom tariffs on the HS system.
- **ProClass**: is a procurement classification system owned by the English local government. Eight of the nine English regions actively support ProClass and an increasing number of authorities across the UK are implementing it in some way. A mapping with the UNSPSC is available.[2]
- **Standard International Trade Classification (SITC)**: is a classification of goods used to classify the exports and imports of a country to enable comparison among different countries and years. The classification system is maintained by the United Nations. The SITC is recommended only for analytical purposes—it is recommended that trade statistics are collected and compiled in the Harmonized System instead.

---

[2] Source: http://proclass.org.uk

- **United Nations Standard Products and Services Code (UNSPSC):** was jointly developed by the United Nations Development Program (UNDP) and Dun & Bradstreet Corporation in 1998 and is currently managed by GS1 (also responsible for GPC), which is responsible for overseeing code change requests, revising the codes and issuing regularly scheduled updates to the code, as well as managing special projects and initiatives.

The list of classification systems above is only a limited overview. There are several local (e.g. ProClass) and industry specific (e.g. ETIM) initiatives. After a period of proliferation, different initiatives are now being mapped and merged. The **two most popular** systems seem to be **Global Product Classification** and **eClass.** Several PIM systems support these standard classification systems off the shelf or can import them.

4.3.4   Complex Attribute Definition

Apart from the simple kinds of attributes already discussed in Sect. 3.3.5, there are also more complex kinds of attributes. Below the main structure of characteristic values, a substructure of additional characteristics can be added.

Tires are a good example of products that have more complex attributes. Fuel efficiency indicates how fuel efficient a tire is. However, fuel efficiency differs according to outside temperature and load. The same applies to other attributes of a tire such as grip and rolling noise. This information can be translated into a table, graphs or other visualization.

Other complex attributes may include 3D models and even CAD/CAM drawings.

4.4   Unit of Measurement Management

As discussed in Sect. 3.3.6, units can be used to define the measurement of a product and for automatic conversion of metric systems and packaging, e.g. in pieces, blisters and pallets. Most PIM systems support the management of unit types, however the extent to which differs widely.

4.4.1   Standard Units

All PIM systems support standard units types such as:
- Length: mm, cm, dm, km, . . .
- Weight: g, kg, t
- Etc.

Even for these kind of units, it has to be determined which definition has to be assigned to a value. Of course this is obvious for "meter" (at least in most European countries). But when a text mentions a 'ton', it has to be clear what it means exactly:

1,000 kilo or 100,000 euros? Likewise, different countries use different definitions for the same words, for instance with regard to the term "pound" (currency, weight).

4.4.2 Custom Units

Companies have a need to define their own units. CRH Construction Materials for example has defined several units to define a number of products in its assortment (See the CRH case in Sect. 8.4):
- A cubic meter of firewood: How many stumps does a cubic meter contain approximately? What is the size of these stumps?
- A "grip" of stones: How many stones are loaded by one "snatch" of a crane machine, 800 or 1,000?

4.4.3 Unit Conversions

Finally, conversions are needed. Simple conversions can be from centimeters to inches or the other way around. Custom units can also include conversions like how many "grips of stone" are needed to build a wall 10 m long, 8 high and 30 cm deep.

PIM systems often use the unit management features to support different currencies. This means that companies have to be able, for example, to convert euros into US dollars on the fly, keeping in mind past and current exchange rates. Unit management can also help here. Other systems use price management to support currencies.

4.5 Catalog and Assortment Management

Catalogs were discussed in Sect. 3.3.1. Companies can create different catalogs for numerous reasons:
- For customer segments;
- For seasons (summer, winter, etc.);
- For specific projects;
- And more.

Each of these catalogs has to be maintained, synchronized with the base catalog and eventually archived.

4.5.1 Catalog Maintenance

From the highest level category that includes the complete product offering, the PIM system is used to provide definitions for sub-catalogs. Every catalog has to be defined: name, version, description, definition and, if applicable, allocation to target groups.

The definition of a sub-catalog determines its basic content. Which product categories are part of the sub-catalog and which are not. Next, the marketing/sales department can make decisions about adding or removing individual products and/or sub-categories. They may even decide to create a new categorization tree.

Catalog management involves several challenges:

- **Time and access management**: the summer catalog must only be available to the public from a certain date onward, but for its production, employees need to have access to the catalog in order to enrich products much earlier.
- **Error reporting**: with regard to products that are no longer available in the base catalog, an alert has to be created so that an alternative can be selected.
- **Versioning**: last year's summer catalog must be kept for back-up, look-back and legal purposes, while a copy of the summer catalog may be used for this year and be adapted to the new summer trends.

4.5.2 Catalog Synchronization

Companies that decide to issue different catalogs with different collections aimed at different target groups, soon have to maintain hundreds of catalogs. A synchronization system is needed as the products in the base catalog change continuously (not only their data but also availability, prices, etc.).

For example, a summer catalog contains a wide variety of swimwear, while a limited part of that category is also included in the winter catalog. You do not want to "copy" each product manually into the new catalog. It is more efficient to create a set of business rules (e.g. all Brand X products within the category Swimwear for Men) and have the copying done automatically.

Likewise, if a supplier adds his new catalog to the PIM system, users have to be able to import the new one and map it with the previous one so that all the previous work of categorization, classification and enrichment can be re-used. However, there should be an option to keep the old catalogs to monitor price and assortment changes.

Synchronization of catalogs includes issues such as:

- **Synchronization Mapping**: when a new catalog is created it has to be possible to define which categories and products are copies.
- **Exception management**: if the base catalog is changed, should the "copy" also change. It may be the case that the product is officially no longer sold but exceptions are made for a good customer.
- **Catalog comparison**: at one time or another catalogs may have to be compared to understand what the differences are (and if different versions are still needed).

Synchronization can be organized in different ways:

- Manually;
- Manually, based on rule-based definitions;
- In a planned way, based in a date structure;
- In a planned way, based in new product selections;
- Log reports;
- By comparing old and new values.

Synchronization can be very complex. Changes in the base catalog can have huge impacts on sub-catalogs. For example, if a product tree is changed in the base catalog, should the new structure be used in all sub-catalogs or not? And if not, how do you map the new structure to the existing structure used in the sub-catalogs?

4.6   Data Quality Management

In Sect. 4.1 I explained that organizations have a need for high quality product data.

Data quality can be supported in various ways. The first step begins by ensuring that only good, properly structured data can be entered by defining attributes well. Which kind of values can be entered? E.g. only even numbers or numbers with an minimum of two digits after the decimal point? Should the name of a product always be in capitals or does only the first letter have to be a capital (to prevent differences in, for example, the name of the brand: Philips or PHILIPS).

In addition to making sure data is entered correctly, highly product technical skilled staff is one of the factors with which many problems can be prevented. Many problems can be avoided if staff really understand the product range and know what information is relevant to its users.

However, the fact is that one can rarely start completely fresh. Product data is sometimes decades old, or imported from outside the organization, or is a collection of several company mergers etc.

Several tools are available for improving product data quality.

4.6.1   Definition of Search Queries

Queries can be defined to detect data errors and anomalies:
• List all products for which no value has been entered for the product name (or any other field);
• List all products for which no alternative product has been assigned;
• List all products for which no product photo is available;
• List all products that have not been assigned to a product category.

Of course the queries stated above are simple examples. A more complex query can be "List all products of which at least one mandatory field has not been filled".

4.6.2   Definition of Reports and Scheduling

Reports can be created based on the queries stated above. The reports can be used as dashboard tools to get an overall view of the product data quality. The queries can also be run every night and be used as a signaling function for staff to start improving product data quality in specific product categories.

For example: the product manager receives an alert when less than 98 % of products have not been assigned to a product category. Reports and queries can be executed on demand or scheduled and its results be forwarded to a specific user or user group.

4.6.3   Log and Error Handling

Error logs give an overview of changes made to the data and errors that occurred and may require correction.

This feature is particularly handy when a lot of product data is imported from sources during the night. A supplier may have changed the data format in which product information is provided, or use different color codes for its new product line.

Most PIM systems have error logging but not all have a signaling function if imports have gone wrong. In addition, error logs are sometimes deeply hidden in the system and require technical expertise. Good error handling systems not only make sure errors are easily seen by the PIM staff, but the PIM staff can also act easily upon it by, for example, initiating a rollback of the product data import from last night and redo the import manually.

4.6.4   User Change Control

It has to be decided which employees can change which information (see also Sect. 4.10).

More advanced PIM systems also log all changes made in the product data, when and by which user, allowing the administrator to monitor the work of his staff and do rollbacks if needed.

4.7   Product Lifecycle Management

The lifecycle of a product determines if and how the product is presented to the customer.

An example of this is a lifecycle based on an alphabetical code:
- A = new product, not yet on the market, cannot be purchased.
- B = new product, not yet on the market, cannot be pre-ordered.
- C = product in the market, can be ordered.
- D = product in decline, sales going down.
- E = do not purchase anymore, but do still sell.
- F = product is no longer purchased nor sold but still in service.
- G = product is no longer purchased nor sold nor in service.

Maintaining the lifecycle of a product allows finer control over several business processes:

- Products with status B may be displayed and pre-ordered, but not yet delivered.
- Products with status D are automatically shown in the "Discount" category.
- Products with status E are no longer sold stand alone but can be ordered as replacement. For instance, customers may want to reorder a lens cap for a camera that has been discontinued for some time.
- Products with status F do not appear in the search results of the Web site in general, only in the search results of the service pages so that customers can download manuals.

The lifecycle of a product can be much further detailed to support workflow processes as well.

4.8   Publication Management

The role of publication management is different from that of catalog management. Catalog management is geared towards the target group. The goal of publication management is to manage the publication of a specific catalog to a specific channel whether print, online etc. (see also Sect. 1.5.2).

Publication management is a useful tool for organizing the production and distribution of publications. The number of different publications may increase quite quickly. For example, LeenBakker, a furniture retailer, issues 26 different brochures per year, in three different languages in two countries and three languages (in the Netherlands in Dutch and in Belgium in Flemish and French). In short, over 78 different publications. This does not include the national and local flyers, and posters that LeenBakker also creates dozens of times a year.

Publication management covers several steps:
- **Publication definition**: when is the process of a specific publication started, when should the publication be approved, printed and when does the publication end (e.g. when are the discounts mentioned in the publication no longer valid)? Which internal users are involved?
- **Publication assortment**: which catalog(s) are part of the publication, how are the products organized in the publication?
- **Publication pricing**: which prices and promotions apply? Should the publication have a separate promotion code so that results can be evaluated?
- **Template Management**: which publication templates (layouts for pages, categories, products) are used?
- **Publication Generation**: How is the publication created?, Which technical format is used (e.g. xml, CSV, PDF) and how is its creation triggered (manually, scheduled), etc.?

Publication management will be further discussed in Chap. 5 which looks at PIM to Print. However, publication management is not only meant to create print publications, it can also be used to create exports for different Web sites, affiliate networks and online marketplaces.

4.9   Product Localization and Translation

Products have to be adapted to suit local situations in two ways:
- **Translation** may be required. It has been proved over and over again that providing product information in the local language can increase conversion up to 50 % and more. Translation is however more than just translating a text. It also implies localizing it to suit local customer needs, focusing, for example, on product strengths that are more valued in one local culture than in another.
- **Localization** means adapting the overall assortment to local needs and cultural differences. This may cover a wide range of product attributes. The product categorization may be optimized as certain products are not sold in a specific region or the way the customer searches differs. However, even specific product photos may convert better in some countries than in others. Even new media assets may be required. For example, quality certificates are considered essential for many products if you try to sell them in Germany, whereas other cultures value design or price more.

Translation and localization can be done on several levels:
- A **master language**, English for example, is used as the common denominator in those countries where sales volume is low and increases in sales are not considered a priority.
- A **region language**, for example German, can cover several different countries.
- A **local language**, for example Swiss German, is supported when the costs outweigh the benefits.
- A **hyper local language**, for example Rhaeto-Romanic (spoken is a small part of Switzerland), is usually only supported when legally mandatory or specific parts of the assortment are targeted at the specific customer segment.

Nikon uses this structure to manage the annual translation and localization of its 80 new products across 35 different countries in Europe (see the Nikon case in Sect. 8.7). The new product is first translated from Japanese into English and validated. The work is then divided across two translation agencies as well as Nikon's local sales organizations. These organizations first translate the product information into regional languages (e.g. French or Dutch). For the Belgian market further localization may be done into Flemish (a form of Dutch) and Belgian French. However, depending on the local need, the back-up languages may be used instead: Dutch and French. As the localization process can take months, even for larger markets, English is first used as fall-back language.

The level to which translation and localization services are supported by the PIM system differ widely. Typical features are:
- Workflow features to assign work to (external) translators;
- Screens optimized to do translation work (usually showing the original text on the left and the text to be translated on the right);
- Pre-translation services (usually Google Translate);
- Text highlighting to show changes in the original text so that only that part has to be translated again;
- Archiving of the original texts for comparison and legal purposes;

- Support of standard interfaces which allow texts in the PIM system to be automatically exported to the systems of translation companies like Translation.com or Linebridge and imported back again into the PIM system after completion.

4.10 Authorization and User Management

Nearly all modern PIM systems distinguish between "users" (a person) and "user groups" to which a user belongs. Access and authorization rules are defined for a user group.

Many PIM systems allow very granular definition of access and authorization rules. This is also a "must have" when the number of (external) users is large.

The administrator should be able to define access rights for all concepts of a PIM system (catalogs, categories, products, variants, attributes, units) and functionality (enrichment, workflow, mapping, etc.).

In addition, the authorization should distinguish several different roles:

- **R = Responsible**: those who do the work to achieve the task;
- **A = Accountable**: the person ultimately responsible for the correct and thorough completion of the deliverable or task;
- **C = Consult**: those whose opinions are sought and with whom there is two-way communication.
- **I = Informed**: those who are kept up-to-date on progress, often only on completion of the task or deliverable; and with whom there is just one-way communication.

It is, as a result, possible to assign specific product categories to specific people and make them responsible for those categories, either as editor, owner or user.

4.11 Media Asset Management

Media assets include everything that is not text. This includes photos, CAD/CAM drawings, but also other graphical presentations, such as logos or videos.

These media assets are usually stored in a **Media Asset Management (MAM)** system which may be part of the PIM system or a separate module or system.

Typical functions of MAM system support processes are:

- **Importing**: this may be a manual process where a product photo is linked manually to a specific product or even variant but also an automated process where data is imported via FTP or XML
- **Assignment**: again this process can be either manual or automated. Depending on the media assets name of meta information the product is linked to a PIM item (e.g. a catalog, category, product, variant, attribute, etc.). A simple form of automated assignment is where the photographer manually gives the file name of the photo the same name as the product ID (e.g. 123456.jpg). More advanced

systems where photos are taken in the sequence in which a photo shoot list is created, allow automatic assignment.

- **Conversion**: media assets have to be converted to be displayed correctly via all supported channels. E.g. a RAW photo file needs to be converted to several different resolutions and formats to be used in print, online and mobile channels.
- **Enrichment**: the media asset can be enriched with additional information such as device of capture, date and place of creation, owner, description, name of the model used, photographer, etc. Some MAM systems can even enrich automatically, for example by analyzing the colors and forms used in the photograph e.g. "red dresses".

Most Media Asset Management systems also have workflow features. Most PIM systems only support quite simple processes like a product attribute which shows the status of the product photography:

- Status A: product is to be shown online but does not have a photo;
- Status B: product has to be picked and sent to the photo studio;
- Status C: product has been picked and sent to the photo studio;
- Status D: product has been photographed;
- Status E: product has to be photographed again as the quality of the product photo is insufficient;
- Status F: product photo is ready to be shown online.

Some PIM systems however have extended functionality which allows PIM users to:

- Define photo shooting for a range of (new) products;
- Create lists of related products needed for the photo shoot (combining comparable products makes the process more efficient);
- Determine per product(list) how many (front, back, side, etc.) and which kind of photos need to be made (simple shots, on models, with or without face, etc.).
- Assignment of a photo shoot to a photo studio, photographer and even specific model.

Like localization and translation, photo and video creation is a very laborious and usually continuous process. However, the process complexity is usually underestimated. Therefore most companies after releasing the first version of their PIM system quickly decide to further invest in the optimization and automation of this process to reduce costs.

4.12 Workflow Management

Workflow is essential for managing the quantity of product data continuously added. Workflow features not only make the process more reliable but also more transparent and manageable.

The level to which workflow is supported differs strongly per PIM system. Workflow can be a simple system where tasks can be created and assigned to users. Some of the more advanced implementations support the following features:

- **Workflow Template Management**: allowing for the creation of workflow processes with steps, paths between steps and triggers (when can the next step be started);
- **Notification**: users are not only notified when a task is assigned to them, but tasks are also escalated to other users (if overdue) and managers can get confirmation when a task is completed;
- **Controlling and Reporting**: managers have access to reports about fulfillment states, overdue dates, the productivity of users, etc. Custom reports can also be created e.g. which photographer has to be asked to redo photos the most often;
- **Validation Rules**: definition of rules for validation of completeness and correctness for execution of tasks.

4.13 Supplier Management

Supplier management is mainly the management of supplier data (name, address, contact details, logo, etc.) in the PIM system.

However, much more complex processes can be added. As already stated briefly in Sect. 1.3.2 the same product can be delivered by several suppliers, including wholesalers or brokers. Each supplier can, however, have its own qualities:

- Supplier A delivers the product the fastest;
- Supplier B is the most reliable supplier;
- Supplier C offers the best price;
- Supplier D offers the best product description;
- Supplier D offers the best product photo;
- Etc.

In the PIM system stakeholders can indicate which suppliers enjoy which preferences (and where exceptions are possible). Some supplier management processes include:

- **Supplier Integration**: the addition of supplier and corresponding assortment to the PIM system (without integration into core assortment). This includes set-up of the supplier in the PIM (and possibly also ERP) system, define mapping and validation rules, integration scheduling and assortment definition. The process usually has a strong overlap with the Master Data Process integration with the company's own ERP system.
- **Supplier Data Update Process**: shows changes in the supplier's assortment: which products are added, changed or removed. Alerts can be defined if large differences are identified in assortments or price differences reach a certain threshold.
- **Supplier Content Integration**: business rules can be defined—which supplier information is used when but also to which supplier an order is sent based on margin, stock availability, or a different supplier characteristic.

4.14   Price Management

Prices are one of the core information elements of a product. In most cases the final product prices are not calculated in PIM systems. This is done in the TILL, ERP or e-commerce system. However, the underlying rules and information pieces can be managed in the PIM system. These can be purchasing prices, discount groups, taxes, recycling fees, etc.

Some of activities the price management processes covers include:

- **Price History Management**: price changes (purchase, gross or sales) should result in creating a new price row with a start- and end-date instead of overwriting existing ones. This allows users to track price history. To keep the system clean, there should be a mechanism to archive price history older than a defined timeframe. However, even archived prices should remain available in one way or another so that all historical price changes can be viewed.
- **Margin Control**: reports, queries and checks need to be implemented to control purchase price changes in relation to sales prices. This is usually ERP functionality but may be implemented in PIM systems to cover non-sufficient ERP systems. The product manager should receive an alert when a vendor comes with a price adjustment that is not in line with the predetermined periodic increase or specified thresholds.
- **Automatic Price Adjustments**: products with highly variable prices (day prices) cannot be maintained manually. The price for which the product is sold is managed automatically. This can be done based on the day price at which the product is purchased but also based on the materials from which the product is made. Examples include materials with high amounts of valuable materials such as copper, aluminum or gold. The product manager can define business rules for different groups of supplier articles, based, among other things, on the raw metal type it contains in order to manage the business rules for calculating purchasing price changes in the market without depending on supplier import prices. To prevent prices from becoming highly volatile, the product manager can also determine the frequency of these adjustments (daily, weekly, monthly or manually).
- **Currency Definition**: of course conversion factors for currencies have to be managed. The official currency conversions can usually be imported but are not used directly to avoid daily changes in prices. Likewise, business rules can be defined per product or product category to prevent awkward pricing. For example, a conversion may lead to prices like 3.78 € or 465.13 €. Business rules may convert these to 3.75 € and 465 €.

4.15   Product Enrichment

The process of adding information to products that is not imported and part of the master data is referred to as product enrichment. This process describes the filling of values for marketing relevant attributes and information (see Sect. 3.1). The main processes of product enrichment are, of course, adding data, either manually or by importing it from third party sources, to products. Some special features some PIM systems offer are:

- **Product comparison**: product managers will often be confronted with products that seem to be the same. In order to see differences (or determine whether the products actually are the same) products need to be compared and their differences preferably highlighted.
- **Simple product relations**: one of the key functions of product enrichment to create relationships between products:
  - Show **similar** or **alternative** products to the product shown;
  - **Up-sell** more expensive products;
  - **Cross-sell** related accessories to a product;
  - Explain that a product **consists of** multiple other products;
  - Offer **spare parts** for a product;
  - **Replace** an old product with a new product;
  - Make it **mandatory** to sell a product bought with another one;

  Product relations can be one-way or two-way, meaning the relationship created applies both ways.
- **Advanced product relations**: creating product relations manually soon becomes too much work. E.g. a product assortment of 10,000 where you want to at least up-sell, cross-sell and show an alternative product, involves creating 30,000 relationships if the relationships are not two-way. Therefore most PIM systems allow editors to define business rules to create product relationships. For example:
  - If product X is not in stock show the next highest priced product in the same category as an alternative;
  - Cross-sell a product from category X with the highest margin product of category Y.

  Some PIM systems even allow transaction data to flow back into the PIM system to create business rules based on purchase behavior (e.g. cross sell the product most sold with this product in the same transaction).
- **Keyword management**: keywords, or tags, can be added to a product. Keywords describe the key elements of a product. For example "T-shirt, red, classic". However one wants to avoid different words being used to describe the same thing e.g. "t-shirts" instead of "T-shirt". Keyword management maintains the list of keywords that editors are allowed to use.
- **Temporary attributes**: certain product attributes may only be valid for a specific period of time. For example, certificates for a product are valid within a certain timeframe (e.g. 1st of January 2014 through 31st of December 2014). During this timeframe it is allowed to present the product together with the given certificate and related medias (logos, certification PDF).

4.16   Mass Mutation

Mass mutation can actually be considered part of the product enrichment process. However, the process is so important that it deserves special attention.

The more products a company manages, the greater the need to modify several products at once. For example, the color of a product and all its variants have to be changed from "Red" to "Limestone Red", or 100 products have to be assigned to a new product category. Some key features of mass mutation include:

- **Filtering for Mass Mutation**: the PIM system should provide a filter for the assortment and filter it down to the selection desired, including the ability to manually add/remove products from this filtered selection.
- **In System Mass Mutation:** ideally the mutation of the filtered selection can be done within the system. All elements of a product should be editable, not only its attribute values but also its relationships, media assignments, etc.
- **Export/Import Mass Mutation:** each PIM system should be able to export/ import data on product and variant level. However, this feature is usually sold as a solution when mass mutation in a system is not supported in very user-friendly way.
- **Rollback Mass Mutations**: the system should make it possible to rollback the changes made by a mass data import.
- **Change Report Generation**: the system should make it possible to generate a report that shows the changes applied to the PIM content by the mass mutation.

The usability of the PIM system for product enrichment is perhaps one of the most important features of a PIM system. Several PIM projects have struggled with what is called the **Spreadsheet Paradigm.** End-users have often maintained product information in a spreadsheet. This system is so easy to use that most PIM systems cannot compete with them. As a result, end-users tend to stick with their spreadsheets, using the export/import features of a PIM system to keep working with the old software. This process is extremely sensitive to errors being made, and should be discouraged.

4.17   Data Import/Export Management

Core functionality of a PIM system is the integration and exporting of data from and to different sources. The system should make it possible to:

- **Select** a catalog to export or import and, if needed, further **filter** the assortment within the catalog to be exported to a publication.
- **Create a mapping** by defining the source and target attributes of the different formats and store the mapping in the PIM.
- **Define conversions** between attributes in an export mapping by specifying rules (for example, in a script language).
- **Define validation rules** to be applied, e.g. to which rules should the data to be imported adhere and how should the system respond if the rules are not met. For example, if the value of a specific field should be within the range "−5" and "5"

and the value in the cell is "100", should the value simply not be entered or should the entire product not be imported?

- **Schedule** an export or import for certain times (continuous, batch, ad hoc) according to the defined interface (eMail, FTP, Web service).

Data import/export is a crucial process that is often part of many other processes in a PIM system (master data, localization, etc.).

PIM to Print

5

5.1 The Death of Print?

As a result of the meteoric rise of digital media, many have prophesied the death of print. But so far this has not been the case. Wholesalers, retailers, production companies, travel agencies all still rely heavily on print as a communication channel. Some examples:

- Thomas Cook creates 17,500 pages for its travel brochures every year.
- Ikea ships its catalog to an estimated 210 million households yearly.
- Fabory publishes an annual catalog with over 80,000 fastener products.
- DIY retailer Praxis distributes a folder almost every week with offerings to millions of households.

Print is not dead, and publishing and distribution of print publications is still an essential part of many marketing departments.

5.2 Printing Process Challenges

The production of print is a complex and time-consuming process. In the traditional way in which catalogs, brochures or leaflets are composed, many different disciplines are involved, each with their own unique way of working.

5.2.1 Unclear Responsibilities

Several departments are involved in the publication of catalogs, flyers, brochures, in-store point of sale material, etc. To take the travel brochure as an example:

- The **marketing department** decides on the layout of the brochure. Which travel destinations get attention? And how many pages are reserved for each destination?

J. Abraham, *Product Information Management*, Management for Professionals,
DOI 10.1007/978-3-319-04885-7_5, © Springer International Publishing Switzerland 2014

- The **purchasing department** decides which accommodation per destination receives extra attention.
- The **design studio** has to make an attractive presentation of the accommodation. If no illustration is available, the studio has to request a photographer to create an attractive picture.
- **Translation agencies** will have to present information in multiple languages.
- The **sales department** may have special wishes in order to sell the products to retailers and consumers better.
- **Other departments** may be responsible for the actual production and distribution of the printed products.

As a result, printing a brochure or catalog becomes a process with many stakeholders and few who feel responsible for the entire process.

5.2.2   Cumbersome Process

In most companies a print process looks something like this:
- Marketing determines on an annual basis when and how often a print publication is created.
- A few months prior to publication, marketing determines how many pages are available in total.
- Purchasing and marketing together determine how many pages each product category should be given.
- Each category purchaser is assigned a set of pages to fill.
- For each page the purchaser lists the products he wants to show on the page and how much of the page space should be used.
- The print coordinator then sets about collecting the name, product description, base and discount price and photo for each product.
- The DTP team (often an external party) creates the layout for each page and enters all product information manually.
- For those products for which no photo is available, a request is sent to the central warehouse or supplier to pick the product and send it to the photo studio.
- The photo studio takes the desired photo and sends it to the DTP team.
- The DTP team creates a low resolution PDF file of each page and sends it to the marketing, print and purchase departments for validation.
- Each PDF page is checked for mistakes. Corrections are often entered by pen on a printout. The printout is faxed back to the DPT team.
- The DTP team corrects any mistakes and creates the final print publication in a high resolution file suitable for printing.
- The entire file (usually several gigabytes of data) is sent to a printing company to be printed.

Apart from the departments listed above, many different stakeholders are usually involved in the process. The costs of creating one print publication may involve several hundreds or even millions of euros. The company's management team wants to have some influence on the end result, as a large print campaign may determine the annual profit or loss of the company. Sales usually believe they are better than Purchasing at knowing what the customer wants. International companies also have to call on the services of translation agencies.

Numerous issues can frustrate the already cumbersome process above:

- When product information is not stored centrally, a considerable amount of time is spent on finding the correct product descriptions, prices, etc;
- As product information is entered manually, mistakes are made;
- Prices and product availability change all the time, and as a result product information has to be updated during the process.
- Similarly, products have to be taken out as they cannot be delivered in time or stock has run out. Cases have been heard of where a catalog has been printed in which up to 25 % of the products were not available for sale.
- Incorrect prices can cost a lot of money and create distrust among customers, particularly if prices come from different departments. These errors are unfortunately still quite common.
- The purchasing and marketing departments are always busy. As a result, input is not delivered on time and validations are made too late, stalling the entire process.
- The number of correction cycles between purchasing, marketing and the DTP team increases as the quality of the product information and control over the process diminishes. Some companies have over 15 correction cycles for each print publication.
- The image quality is poor as the images are found on the fly and created in different ways. Similarly, they are made over and over again as the company has no single source for storing the images.

5.3   PIM Systems in the Printing Processes

Several PIM systems have features that support the print creation process. A PIM system helps to track deadlines and escalate automatically if necessary. This ensures that jobs are done on time.

First of all the PIM system offers the different stakeholders in the process one source of truth regarding product information and media assets. This removes several issues surrounding finding the right product data and photos.

A second feature that PIM systems support is the creation of print publications and page templates (see Fig. 5.1). The number of pages can be set for each print publication. A template can be assigned to each page from a fixed set of templates. This results in a publication plan.

With the workflow feature that several PIM systems have, purchasers can then be assigned their set of pages. For each page they only have to determine which product to show where. The benefit of working from a system also allows better control over who has done what and who is late and where.

Several PIM systems allow the pages to be filled on the fly. Based on the article ID, all necessary information is retrieved from the PIM and placed in the template.

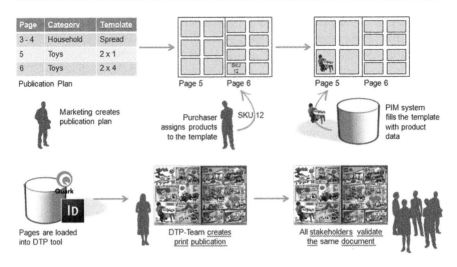

Fig. 5.1 The PIM 2 print process (*Source*: Unic)

Discussions can already be held about which product should be placed where, based on a temporary result.

The pages can then be exported to DTP tools like Adobe Indesign or Quark Express. The designers here can fine tune the page designs and add non-product related text and visuals like articles and advertisements.

As soon as the designer saves the document, the PDF preview for the person responsible for the product is updated. He receives an alert and can now check whether all corrections have been made. It is also possible to include more people (specialists) in the workflow with fewer errors along the way.

The PIM system can even support the correction cycle which is usually a ping-pong of remarks on tens of pages. Several PIM systems make it possible to store PDF files created by the designer in the PIM systems. Remarks can be entered in the PDF by all stakeholders, allowing discussions to take place in one document and on one page. The remarks can be imported into the design tool. The designer has the remarks right on the spot should he need to make changes.

Some PIM systems even have an option to import data from the DTP tool, back into the PIM system. For example, a mistake in the product name can be corrected in the DTP tool and then imported back into the PIM system.

In short, the PIM system makes it possible to have one unique source of product information throughout the entire process. The person responsible for product information can maintain the information and be sure that this information is printed correctly. If there are product information errors, they can be corrected in the PIM system and automatically updated in the DTP document. This is a big advantage as the maintenance process is decoupled from the design process.

In addition, it is also possible in the PIM system to streamline the image shooting, preparation and approval process, and the conversion into the required formats for the different channels (see Media Asset Management in Sect. 4.11).

Fig. 5.2 How many weeks are needed to create a catalog (with or without PIM)? *Source*: Heiler PIM ROI Study, 2011

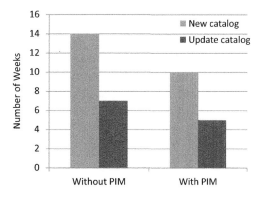

Fig. 5.3 How many print catalogs do you publish annually including language variants? *Source*: Heiler

5.4 PIM to Print Benefits

The benefits of using a PIM system to support the print process have been researched by several companies. According to Heiler the **throughput time** of creating a print catalog can be reduced by 30 % (see Fig. 5.2).

The expected **cost reduction** depends on the starting situation. A cost reduction of up to 50 % is possible when production has been done entirely manually. A large number of people are no longer needed when the processes are streamlined and the number of correction cycles are reduced to a minimum.

Cost reduction has the greatest impact in the design department, as most of the processes that are done without a PIM system are now automated and streamlined. This means that fewer people can do the same amount of work. There are also other, more usual, benefits that are not calculated, i.e. having better product information and better images.

As already stated in Sect. 2.3.2 the costs savings are often not achieved. Instead the number of print publications is increased and more tactical and strategic benefits are achieved (see Fig. 5.3).

For example, PIM to print diminishes the risk that incorrect product information is printed and products are offered that are not available.

Likewise, PIM to print also enables the company's sales personnel, customers and trading partners to easily create marketing materials to suit local needs while giving company officials the content control needed to maintain brand consistency. These materials can then be printed locally by the resellers themselves or the distributor can print them on their customers' behalf using one of their pre-approved commercial printers. As a result, print is becoming increasingly more customized, even as far as a 1 to 1 communication medium.

Selecting a PIM System

6

This chapter examines the different options for developing a PIM system, the different PIM system suppliers and the process involved in selecting a PIM system.

6.1   Build or Buy

Should you license a commercial product that meets 80 % of your needs but offers a lot more complexity due to additional features that you do not need. Or would it be better to build your own system, one that meets all your requirements without the unnecessary features?

According to a study by Heiler Software, a significant proportion (27 %) of companies work with a PIM/MDM environment that they have developed themselves.[1] However, in many cases these systems were developed in the last century before the actual rise of PIM systems. They are often extensions of (custom) ERP systems or database-driven publishing systems. According to the same study, 60 % of this "Build yourself" group is no longer satisfied with their current PIM system and require improvements or expansion.

The main reasons for developing software in-house are the ability to customize the software to a company's own processes. The idea that developing software in-house might also be cheaper has, in recent years, already proven, in most cases, to be wrong. Generally speaking, the buy versus build choice can be made by stating that standard processes should be using standard software. Standard software allows for a shorter time to market and generally lower maintenance costs. Core competence, competitive distinguishing processes should be IT supported in-house.

Based on our experience the current generation of PIM systems **no longer** have any room to follow a **"fully fledged build strategy"**. Nearly all **PIM systems allow**

---

[1] "ROI of Product Data for Multichannel Commerce", Heiler Software AG and the Stuttgart Media University, 2012, the study can be ordered at: http://www.pim-roi.com

J. Abraham, *Product Information Management*, Management for Professionals,   73
DOI 10.1007/978-3-319-04885-7_6, © Springer International Publishing Switzerland 2014

advanced customization, especially the mature PIM systems discussed in Sect. 6.2. Most PIM systems are built to "blend in" with the existing IT landscape. They have numerous integration features and are very customizable e.g. you can create your own data model. PIM systems can therefore, to some extent, be better compared to standard applications like an Oracle or Microsoft Database. It is on these systems that you build your core competences, not in the systems themselves.

In order to be complete, price is also no longer an argument for internal development. There are PIM systems in **several price ranges** from open source to multi-million corporate systems that cover the needs of small local, online only production companies, to large international multichannel wholesalers and retailers. The pricing models of most vendors has also become more flexible, making it possible to determine where the costs should lie, more on the OPEX or the CAPEX side. Finally, several PIM parties offer SAAS solutions, allowing for lower maintenance costs.

In general **only** the "**buy and integrate**" or "**buy, integrate and customize**" strategy can be considered valid choices. Following a "buy strategy" does not imply that no development work will be required. Integration with different sources and channels will be needed. Adaptation of source systems is often needed to allow the export of data to the PIM system. Configuration of the PIM system is also required to meet the specific processes and information demands of the organization.

However, according to a study by Ventana Research, 41 % of participants in larger organizations reported that they develop custom code.

6.2   Supplier Overview

While research companies like Gartner and Forrester evaluate many different systems, including MAM and MDM, they have not yet evaluated PIM systems specifically. Ventana is the only research company that evaluates PIM systems on a regular basis.[2]

Figure 6.1 lists the PIM systems evaluated by Ventana Research. The analsysis by Ventana Research is not intended to imply that one vendor or product is the right choice for all companies. They tend to provide a baseline of knowledge that organizations can use to evaluate vendors and products.

Ventana's definition of PIM systems also differs slightly from the one used in this book. Whereas we limit a PIM system to managing marketing related product information, Ventana extends the reach of a PIM system across the enterprise supply chain for the entire product lifecycle.

The evaluation below is based on Ventana Research's scoring on five product-related criteria: usability, manageability, reliability, capability, and adaptability. In

[2]*Ventana Research Value Index: Product Information Management in 2011* (http://www. ventanaresearch.com/).

Fig. 6.1 PIM systems
evaluated by Ventana
Research

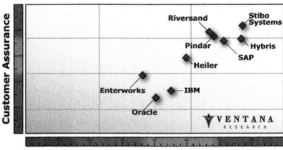

The Ventana Research Value Index: 2011
Product Information Management

addition, Ventana Research also included two customer assurance categories: vendor validation and total cost of ownership and return on investment (TCO/ROI).

In Chap. 9 we discuss several of the vendors listed by Ventana Research and several others in more detail.

There are many other PIM or PIM related suppliers in addition to the ones mentioned by Ventana Research, including:

- **Adam Software**: originates from the DAM area towards PIM and other Marketing campaigning and publication processes.
- **Apsiva**: offers a suite of software products for the creation and maintenance of print, Web, and electronic catalogs.
- **Perfion**: based in Denmark, Perfion offers a broad solution covering PIM, PLM, e-commerce, Web content management, PIM to Print and integration tools.
- **PIMcore**: an open source CMS and PIM system based on PHP.
- **Imperia/Pirobase**: started as CMS provider and expanded into the PIM field.
- **MDC/Katalogmanagement.de**: offers a PIM, DAM and newsbuilder.

There are also several players who focus on PLM but also offer some PIM features e.g. Actify, Altair Engineering, Aras Corp, Arena Solutions, Autodesk, Centric Software, Dassault Systems, Geometric, Gerber Technology, IFS, Infor, Lectra, Omnify Software, Oracle, Parametric Technology Corp. (PTC), SAP, Selerant, Siemens and Visual 2000.

Finally, several parties, mainly MDM solution providers, offer tools that cover some of the PIM processes discussed, including Dataflux, GSX, Informatica, Information Builders, Liaison Technologies, Orchestra Networks, Microsoft, Pervasive, Talend, Teradata, Tibco Software, TIE Commerce, and Zynapse.

6.3   The PIM Selection Process

A selection process for a PIM system is no different from that of any other business process software. As with the choice for an ERP or CRM system, it requires time and effort to select the right software vendor and integrator. We would like to share a few tips in this section.

Although we are stating the obvious, we have all too often seen that companies base their requirements on the feature lists of software vendors. As a result features that are not really needed become "must haves". In addition, the feature list from the vendor who came in first often wins as their list creates the frame of reference for evaluating the others.

We therefore recommend a different approach.

6.3.1   Create a Decision Making Unit (DMU)

Form a team of all stakeholders involved in your organization (for a list of users see Sect. 1.4). Also include ICT to make sure that the technical quality of the system can be validated. Keep the team small (5–6 people) and consisting of actual users and experts. If necessary, create a steering committee to which the DMU reports for management buy-in and financial backing.

6.3.2   Do Not Speak to Vendors

Agree within the DMU not to speak to vendors. After reading this book you will know more about PIM than most sales representatives of PIM software vendors. All good sales people will try to adapt your decision-making framework to the functionality their systems offer. Create your own first.

6.3.3   Create Your Own Feature List

Use the processes described in Chap. 4 to determine which processes actually need to be supported. Determine the priority per feature. The MOSCOW methodology works fine if you give it a value:
- 0 = "Not needed"
- 1 = "Would have"
- 2 = "Could have"
- 4 = "Should have"
- 0 = "Must have features".

Be careful with making features mandatory "must haves". If a system cannot provide a mandatory feature, it should be kicked out.

6.3.4   Think Out-of-the-Box

Consider which other business processes you might want to cover with the new system. Do product lifecycle management or e-commerce processes play an important role? Add them to your feature list. It may also help in getting more sponsors and financial resources for the project.

6.3.5   Include Other Criteria

Apart from the functional match, which is based on your feature list, there are several that can be added:

- **Customer satisfaction:** try to ask for references to assess their customer satisfaction. You can use the Net Promotor Score (NPS) methodology for this.[3] You only have to ask one question: "Would you recommend this vendor to your family and best friends" where "0 = It is extremely unlikely I will ever recommend this vendor" and "10 = It is extremely likely I will recommend this vendor". The percentage of positive references (9 or 10) are added up and the percentage of negative references (6 or lower) are discounted, leading to the NPV score. Of course the number of references is usually insufficient to really calculate the NPV but asking the question might be a good start for a discussion e.g. why an eight and not a nine. Include the results in your evaluation but consider the tips given in the separate section "Do not trust references of vendors".
- **Organizational match:** this criteria is highly subjective. What it means to do is assess whether the vendor (and its integrator) match with your organization. Typical matches where you know you can expect trouble is when a small local manufacturer tries to work with a global PIM system integrator or a formalized, highly hierarchical retailer signs a covenant with an agile, new PIM software company.
- **Total cost of ownership (TCO):** attempt to translate the pricing models of the different vendors into one uniform amount; the TCO per year that includes all costs categories (see also Sect. 7.2). Capital expenditure costs are to be spread across multiple years. The number of years depends on your company's financial policy but in our experience it should at least be 5–7 years. PIM systems are becoming mature and there is no longer a need to change them rapidly as is the case of, for example, e-commerce systems. Of course TCO also serves as kick-out criteria, as the company has to be able to pay for the system and the business case should be able to carry the investment.
- **Vendor reliability:** again a kick-out criteria. Is the vendor financially healthy? Is it likely to be bought by a larger software vendor. The last question is almost as important as the first. We have all too often seen that acquisition of a software

---

[3] Source: http://en.wikipedia.org/wiki/Net_Promoter

vendor stops software development for a period of 1 or 2 years while the company is integrated and old staff and management leave the organization.

We explicitly did not add as criteria "match with IT architecture". Most PIM systems' core is integration with other systems. The fact as to whether it is based on the same technology standards as other core applications of the company therefore becomes less relevant unless the ICT department would like to do part of the development and maintenance of the system in-house.

6.3.6   Rank Your Criteria List

Which criteria are really important? Try to give each criteria a weight. An example weighting could be:

- Functional match: 60 %
- Customer satisfaction: 20 %
- Organizational match: 20 %
- Total Cost of Ownership: 10 %
- Vendor reliability: 10 %

Do Not Trust References of Vendors
In our opinion the value of references can be huge if reference research is done well. Most of the time the **software vendors provide references** from two or three user organizations. **Don't call them**. The ones provided will always be positive for several reasons. First of all, the software vendor knows they are happy with the software. They are likely to be his happiest customers. They are by no means his average customers.

Secondly, these references are likely to have a long-term, sometimes a very close and friendly, relationship with their software vendor. Even if these users have been confronted with disadvantages, they will be hesitant to mention them as it may harm their relationship.

Thirdly, to some extent, the reference organizations rely on their software vendor for support and service. A vendor that might be willing to implement that long-time desired new feature if the reference company can help get this new customer on board.

Finally, we have seen cases where references are simply bought. Not so much by new features but conferences in sunny destinations or by giving large discounts on implementation and service costs. In some cases, providing positive references is even part of the contract signed between the software vendor and the user organization.

Of course references can still provide very good insights into the supplier's capabilities. Our advice is to request a list of all customers and then call the references that are comparable to your organization in size, processes and market. Do not ask for permission, as you will not get it. It is your right to call another company for a reference for which permission is not needed.

TCO and Vendor reliability may not be given a weight but be treated as kick-out criteria. It is no use evaluating a system that cannot meet the financial resources or business case of the company. Likewise, we strongly recommend NOT to buy software from a vendor that is filing for bankruptcy.

6.3.7   Create a Shortlist

We have seen many companies invite five or more suppliers. In general a person already has a hard time choosing from three options. Please use the list provided in Chap. 4 and the supplier information in Appendix II to create a shortlist.

Ask software vendors to fill in a questionnaire covering your feature list and other selection criteria. Per feature ask if it is supported:

- "out-of-the-box"
- via configuration
- through an integrated partner solution
- through add-on products provided by partners (which ones)
- via modifications (screen configurations, reports, GUI tailoring, etc.)
- via a third party solution
- via customization
- will be supported in a future release
- not supported

If it is not "out-of-the-box", ask for an estimate in additional development hours. In this way you can get a better understanding of the actual implementation effort and total software and integration costs.

6.3.8   Demand an Intensive Demo

We do not recommend only working with questionnaires that ask about the extent to which their software meets the feature list. Most will state they can support all features either straightaway, with only minor customization, or with a very easy to implement third-party product.

Asking the vendor to demonstrate all features on a working system is much more insightful. It not only tells you if the feature is really supported, but also to what extent and how easy it is for users to work with the system. Take at least a day to get to know the system. It is a small investment compared with the amount of money you are likely going to spend on the total project.

6.3.9   Score the Vendors

Have each member of the DMU score the vendors individually. Keep the scoring easy. Give the worst scoring vendor a "1" and the best scoring vendor a "3" for each criteria. Vendors that do not support a mandatory feature should be kicked out. By multiplying the score by the weight you can evaluate each supplier based on its merits in an objective way. Of course it is only the start of an internal discussion but it helps keep things objective until all the facts are on the table.

Implementing a PIM

7

This chapter does not focus on the approach to implementing a PIM. To a large extent implementing a PIM is the same as for any other business process oriented system. The challenges are the same: no real commitment from higher management, lack of internal ICT resources, etc.

This chapter focuses instead on specific steps in the development process of a PIM system where things usually go terribly wrong.

7.1 Creating the Business Case

In Chap. 2 we discussed the business benefits of a PIM system and you can use this chapter as a basis for creating your own business case. However, it may still be difficult to convince management. Therefore a few tips:

- **Don't focus on cost reductions**: in general we see that PIM systems do not reduce costs and they even increase cost visibility. For one, we already stated that PIM systems make it possible to do more in the same amount of time. Secondly, product information management is fragmented prior to the introduction of a PIM system. Costs are hidden across multiple departments. With the introduction of a PIM system companies start to maintain their product data better, increasing the visible costs.
- **Unless you are using the PIM for Print:** one big exception to the statement made above. For print we see a clear measurable benefit of having a PIM system.
- **Focus on strategic and tactical benefits:** such as cost reductions, revenue increases are difficult to measure in practice. There may be several external reasons why conversion and revenue do not increase e.g. an economic downturn. We therefore recommend focusing on the strategic and tactical benefits when building your business case. A long-tail strategy, shorter time to market and legal compliance are, in practice, easier to explain and defend to higher management.
- **Find a business sponsor**: PIM is often IT driven in order to harmonize different systems and create one source of truth for product information. However, the

J. Abraham, *Product Information Management*, Management for Professionals,
DOI 10.1007/978-3-319-04885-7_7, © Springer International Publishing Switzerland 2014

business case for this is often difficult to defend. Try to find a sponsor where the PIM benefits are the clearest: marketing and sales.

• **Create time**: a PIM system not only takes time to implement (from 3 to 12 months or more, depending on the complexity), it also takes time to realize the benefits as employees have to get used to the new processes and the product information has to be enriched and distributed. Make sure "judgment day" is set within a reasonable timeframe, preferably at least 1 year after going live, but preferably 2 years.

7.2   Don't Underestimate the Costs

Asking for more is something Oliver Twist did, but is something you would like to avoid. We have seen too often that the total costs of a PIM project are underestimated. Usually the external software license costs are considered and even the implementation effort by external parties. However, in the sales process other external software needed to make things work e.g. middleware and new version of design software is forgotten. Likewise, the investment needed internally to open up legacy systems to the PIM is often neglected or underestimated.

The list below is an overview of the different cost components (which can either be CAPEX or OPEX based).

Software licenses:
• PIM software
• DAM/MAM software
• Database software
• Middleware software
• Other (OS, Network)

Software implementation:
• PIM side
• Source side
• Middleware

Other customization work:
• PIM system
• DAM/MAM
• Middleware
• Source systems

Hardware and Hosting Services:
• PIM system
• DAM/MAM
• Middleware
• Source systems

Functional Application Maintenance
• PIM system

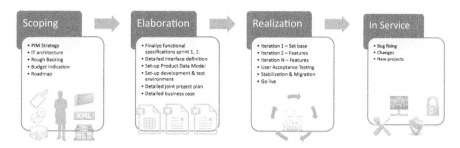

Fig. 7.1 Phased implementation of a PIM system (*Source*: Unic)

- DAM/MAM
- Middleware
- Source systems
  Technical Application Maintenance
- PIM system
- DAM/MAM
- Middleware
- Source systems

It is therefore recommended that management is not asked for a total investment budget for the entire project at the start. Instead we recommend breaking the project up into four phases as illustrated in Fig. 7.1.

The PIM strategy is determined in the **scoping phase**. The PIM strategy states what the company actually wants to achieve with the PIM system. It includes a roadmap of when which PIM sub-project has to be implemented. A typical phasing may, for example, be that all product sources are first unified into one PIM system. From there on a long-tail strategy may be set up, followed at last by a PIM to Print project. We recommend a roadmap to keep the scope of each project small. This allows you to keep the projects manageable and the results visible, but always have a clear end-state.

The end-state must also be clear in order to create good ICT architecture. This may sound obvious but several PIM projects have had to be partly redone because the end-state was unknown to the developers beforehand. One client company for example decided half-way through its first project that it also wanted to use the PIM system for its print processes (it had in the past explicitly stated it did not want to cover this process). PIM to print however requires the storage of very high resolution pictures (up to 50+ Mb per photo). However, this particular company had opted for a "PIM in the cloud" solution based on known requirements. For high volume data storage and traffic this proved the wrong architecture as the cloud solution is both too expensive and too slow for PIM to Print.

The ICT architecture lists which source systems will need to be interfaced with and how, and which channels will have to be supported. It should be designed with the future in mind and define the integration mechanisms, which data to migrate when, which processes and workflows to improve or redesign, estimate the load/volume of data and users, the service levels per region and required ICT skills per region. Based on this information a PIM integrator should be able to give a rough estimate based on earlier projects.

In the **elaboration phase** the functionality for the first project is defined in more detail to get a better understanding of the project complexity. Likewise, the product data model and interfaces are defined. Finally, based on more detail, a detailed project plan and business case can be created for the first project.

We do not believe in trying to estimate all the project costs in great detail. It may be 1–2 years before all sub-projects have been **implemented** and **in service** by which time the organization, and its environment will have changed and, likely, also its business priorities. However, by outlining the long-term strategy, you avoid making architectural choices that hamper these long-term goals.

7.3   Develop Agile . . . to Some Extent

There are several ways to develop a system. The waterfall method is traditionally used. Here all requirements are first defined in detail after which the system is completely built. Only then can the system be tested by end-users and debugged.

The disadvantages of this approach is that is takes months and sometimes years before a system can be tested. During the development period, the organization and the market change as do business requirements and priorities. It may well be the case that a system is developed that is no longer needed or which has to do things differently. Likewise, the developers do not get any feedback on their work. A misunderstanding of the requirements or a wrong architectural choice may lead to a system not meeting business expectations.

In the last decade most parties have come to agree that the waterfall method is not suitable for developing systems where the business and/or technological environment is not stable.

Due to the disadvantages of the waterfall method, a different approach has been gaining in popularity in the last decade: agile development. The key concepts of agile development are[1] (see also Fig. 7.2):

- The entire software process is chopped up into much smaller iterations (also called sprints). These iterations usually have a length of 1, 2 or 3 weeks, depending on the chosen rhythm.
- A complete development cycle is executed within such an iteration, including requirements definition, development, testing and debugging.
- The requirements for the second iteration are determined during the first iteration. The requirements are only fixed just before the development process starts which allows the addition, change and removal of features.

---

[1] Actually agile development is much more than this. If you would like to know more, please visit http://en.wikipedia.org/wiki/Agile_software_development

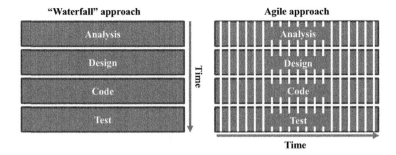

Fig. 7.2 The waterfall versus the agile approach

The agile development approach makes it possible to deliver results faster, get (test) feedback from the business immediately after each iteration, and allows the business to change its mind. As you divide the project into smaller pieces it becomes possible to get better control of the project, as complexity per element drops. It also facilitates the creation of software that meets business requirements better and is of higher quality.

A PIM system is ideal for being developed in iterations as it is easy to develop and test in parts while it can still add value to the business. However, we do not believe in "going completely agile", where no requirements are written before the actual start of the project, for two reasons:

- **Interfaces are developed across development teams**: interfaces often require modification on both sides of the interface. The PIM team can work in an agile manner, but the development team at the source and/or channel system may not be used to working this way. Dependency between the teams should also be kept to a minimum to prevent the project becoming too complex. We therefore recommend that interfaces are defined in detail before the actual development process starts. This allows the teams to work in their own way and independently.
- **The creation of a Product Data Model takes too long**: Sect. 3.5 discussed the creation of a product data model. We believe it is best to start the creation of this model before the actual project and have it complete before the second or third iteration. Firstly, it is mainly a business task to create the product data model. Several PIM systems allow the import of the model from an Excel/CVS file. In other words, business can do the work. Once it is imported, however, and product data entered, changing it has to be done in the PIM system which usually takes more effort. Secondly, it takes a lot of time to create a good product data model. We have seen in several projects that the creation of the product data model takes nearly as long as the development of the PIM system. One reason is simply because it is just a lot of work, but also because a lot of people have to be involved, making the process more cumbersome and political.

7.4   Check Your Data Quality

Data quality is regularly underestimated. Product data is always incomplete, missing, duplicate, obsolete, corrupt or dirty. This is to some extent also to be expected
when the data has been worked with often for more than several decades by tens or
hundreds of people. With the introduction of a PIM system you are making the rules
for good data stronger and bad data becomes more visible.

Some examples of data we came across in the past few years:

- **Duplicate**: the same product has been entered 18 times over the last 10 years by
  different people as no clear validation process existed to check if the product
  already existed in the system.
- **Plain garbage**: the fields are used to maintain information which is definitely not
  meant to be stored in the system. We once found the following text in a product
  description: "NEVER DO BUSINESS WITH THIS SUPPLIER AGAIN".
- **Incomprehensible**: product names are written in a kind of code. Nobody knows
  to which SKU the product name actually refers.
- **Incomplete**: mandatory fields have not always been mandatory or have been
  circumvented by the data entry staff. 35 % all products have at least one
  mandatory field not filled in and can, as a result, not be sold.
- **Inconsistent**: if the material code of a product was unknown, "999" was entered.
  Later on, employees preferred the code "Unknown" or "000". A few years later,
  the field was made non-mandatory. However, old employees kept entering the
  old codes. New employees did not enter any data.
- **Non-conform**: the article ID is not uniform. SKUs may have the same ID or
  updates of the same product are given the same article ID.
- **Inaccurate**: 30 % of the articles in a one million SKU system have not been sold
  for the last 15 years. After analysis, it was decided to archive more than 250,000
  SKUs from the system.
- **Not structured**: there is no categorization within the ERP system for over
  50,000 SKUs while at the same time over 300 product categories exist in the
  ERP system without any products.

The introduction of a PIM system is also the time to clean up the old data, not
only because the old rule applies: "garbage in; garbage out". Dirty data makes
migration of the data into the PIM system impossible. For example, a well set-up
PIM system will refuse SKUs with double article IDs. Likewise, the different
material codes have to be inventoried and mapped to one, correct, material code,
before migration can proceed.

In other words, data cleaning is needed before data migration can start. Data
cleaning is unfortunately a tedious, often lengthy, and to a large extent mainly a
manual task involving the following steps:

- **Data extraction**: data cleaning should never been done directly on the operational systems but on a copy of the operational data to prevent mistakes actually
  hampering operations.

- **Data analysis**: the new data validation rules can be tested on the extracted dataset. There are several commercial and free automated tools that can validate the data.
- **Data prioritization**: in the analysis several kinds of errors will be found as listed above. Some are serious and need to be solved before the data is imported into the PIM system. Others can best be solved in the PIM system itself, while a few are minor issues and can be ignored.
- **Data cleaning**: with the priorities set, there are several specialized companies and tools on the market to assist in data cleaning. However, even managing these external resources can be a job for several people depending on the size of the dataset. Some work can also be left for the PIM system if it has data transformation features.
- **Data validation**: all validations are run again to determine whether all critical data issues have been resolved. Several iterations are usually needed to clean up the data, once the first mistakes have been solved, new ones emerge.
- **Data merging**: if the data is clean the actual migration of data can start. The data is ideally imported in the source system and from there maintained and interfaced with the PIM system. In this way the source is cleaned up as well.
- **Data change implementation**: this step is often forgotten. Cleaning data is not only about technical stuff. It is about educating people as to which data validation rules apply and how product information processes are run. Not explaining, implementing and enforcing the new data rules and processes will result in polluted data the very second the first entry is made in the newly cleaned-up data.

7.5 Migration: Take It Slow

Once your data has been cleaned, you can start the actual migration. The biggest challenge of migration is the moment to switch. A lot of product data is used continuously, so when is a good time to stop working in the old system? There are three general migration scenarios:

7.5.1 Big Bang

In this case implementation happens in a single instance. All users move to the new processes and systems at the same time. Source data is redirected to the new system and channels are fed from the new PIM systems.

The advantage of big bang migrations is that their implementation period is short and costs are lower compared with their alternatives. The pain and issues surrounding any migration is also kept to within a short period of time. People also prefer big bangs from a change management point of view. There is a clear date and deadline and often no turning back.

However, big bang migrations are risky. Data and system issues that were not found during testing may suddenly emerge bringing the business to a halt.

7.5.2 Incremental

A PIM system often allows for incremental implementation. The source systems are usually capable of delivering to multiple systems at the same time. The PIM system is often used first to feed the Web site(s) after which it is slowly introduced for other channels. Other migration paths are, of course, also possible such as introduction per organizational unit, country/language, etc.

Benefits of incremental migration are that risks are less as not all functionality and data are migrated at once. Likewise, users and developers have more time to learn and prevent mistakes down the line.

A disadvantage is that old systems are kept running and people may have to maintain data in two or more systems (which was one of the benefits of introducing a PIM). There is also less feel for urgency which may hinder project progress.

7.5.3 Shadow

Also called parallel migration. Both systems are maintained until the new system has been working sufficiently well to make the final switch. While this approach minimizes risk, the costs are the highest.

Shadow migrations also have a tendency to never stop. We have seen organizations where, even after 4 years, both PIM systems are still maintained because the final improvements allowing the old PIM system to be switched off are never realized.

In practice we see that big bang and incremental migrations are equally the most popular. Shadow migrations are far less popular as they demand running systems in parallel. In our opinion big bang migrations are often the most logical choice when a PIM system is introduced in the organization for the first time. If the system is replacing existing systems, then an incremental approach is recommended.

7.6   Start Product Enrichment as soon as Possible

As cleaning data can be a task that takes months, and in some cases even years of manpower, enriching the product data in accordance with the newly defined product data model is a similarly lengthy process. We usually advise our clients to start the data collection process at the same time as the project is started, even before the start of defining the product data model. The reason for this is simple—enriching data takes a long time and the more products and attributes there are, the longer it takes.

A few tips:

- **Inform suppliers**: tell suppliers about your PIM project. This is also the time to determine which information they can provide, in which formats and also their willingness to provide it.

- **Find additional sources**: as discussed in Sect. 1.5.1, there are many other potential sources for product information which may be able to accelerate your product information gathering process.
- **Build your data PIM team**: for data cleaning and enrichment you need a team that is temporarily larger than your existing product information team. If there is no team yet, you have to build it from scratch (see also Sect. 7.8). It is also possible to source part of this work to lower wage countries, e.g. India. If your base language is not English, you may find a partner in a former colony (e.g. Surinam for the Dutch).
- **Start gathering**: do not wait until the PIM system is finished to add new product information. Companies can usually kick off with an Excel sheet which allows them to start entering data that is later on imported into the PIM system.

It may sound obvious, but we have seen several instances where the PIM system going live was hampered by the fact that the product information enrichment project was not yet completed. In one instance a delay of 6 months led to serious financial damage.

7.7 Governance and Organization

There are two important organizational issues that need to be resolved when starting a project. "Who is responsible?" and "How do we organize the PIM team? ".

7.7.1 Who Is Responsible?

For the PIM project itself the recommendation is to set up a steering committee as nearly all departments are involved some way PIM. Tip: make sure only decision makers with financial and managerial authority are on the steering committee. Work should be done by the team. Decisions should be made in the steering committee.

There is no one single solution for the permanent situation. PIM by nature extends across the organization (see also Sect. 1.4). When PIM is introduced for the first time in the organization, the question arises as to who is responsible for it, and if the question does not arise, then it should be.

In the ROI study by Heiler (see also Fig. 7.3) it is clear that among manufacturers, the responsibility is more clearly in the hands of marketing rather than product management or e-commerce. When comparing the answers given by retailers with and without PIM, 52 % of PIM users say that product management was responsible for PIM and its data quality.

We have seen instances where PIM is managed by purchasing, marketing, sales or ICT. It strongly depends on what the goals of PIM are. The department that is set to gain the most benefits, usually also bears the costs and therefore also gets the responsibility. In the end, for a PIM this is generally the marketing department. Among retailers in particular, we often find the product information management

Who is responsible for product information

Fig. 7.3 Who is responsible for PIM? *Source*: Heiler

team reporting to the marketing director. However, the ICT department often continues to play a major role in the technical and functional more complex aspects of PIM.

7.7.2   How to Organize a PIM Team

In general we see three ways to create a PIM team:

- **Centralized**: while there may be many users who view the product information across the organization, the actually editing is done by a small core team who maintains the data. We see this model in particular in retail companies and smaller organizations.
- **Decentralized**: in this case each department is made responsible for enriching some of the product data. Sales, for example, maintain attributes related to sales, marketing for marketing, logistic for logistics. This model is more popular among production companies where a lot of people are involved in product creation.
- **Hybrid**: sometimes some of the work is delegated while the responsible unit still does most of the work.

In general we are strongly in favor of limiting the flow of product information outside the PIM system to a minimum. When a department has the information about a product, either because it is provided by an external source or because it creates this information itself, the department itself should enter the information directly into the PIM system. Sending emails to a different person who then enters the information is not only inefficient, it is also a way of not taking responsibility for product information.

The following roles can be distinguished in the PIM team:

- **PIM Owner**: independent of which organizational model is chosen, it is essential that one person is made responsible for the overall PIM process. This should be a person in higher management (e.g. e-commerce manager, marketing director) who can serve as escalation channel and business owner for the PIM steward. The responsibilities of the PIM owner are:
  - enforce the PIM system as "single source of truth" for product information.
  - manage the relationship with the content suppliers;
  - determine the development roadmap of the PIM in consultation with other stakeholders in the organization;
  - manage the different ICT suppliers;
  - chair the steering group for the PIM system, if applicable.
- **PIM Steward**: this person is operationally responsible for the overall product information process, the PIM system, and the quality of the product information itself. In some companies this role is fulfilled by the same person responsible for the master data in the ERP system, the data steward. On a daily basis he or she:
  - manages the product data model and the introduction and removal of catalogs, categories, classifications classes, attributes, etc.
  - is the functional administrator of the PIM system and steers functional improvements and expansions (adding new sources and channels).
  - guards the PIM system as "single source of truth" for product information.
  - trains other users in the organization to use PIM.

  The above tasks are often not a full time job and the PIM steward also takes on a role as product specialist. The education level of the PIM stewards should however not be underestimated. A higher education level is needed to understand both the conceptual framework of a product data model as well as understand the intricacies of the company's product assortment.
- **Product analyst/specialist**: depending on the organization, this may be a person whose role is limited mostly to data entry. However, we see that as product information is expanded, this role becomes more and more one for specialists who really know and understand the part of the assortment assigned to him or her. He or she may well be the source in the organization for product knowledge and the third line of support for customer enquiries.

Other roles that may fit into the PIM team are that of product photographer, creative artist, video specialist, etc. However, we see in practice that these roles are often outsourced.

7.8   Change Management

One of the greatest risks in the implementation of a PIM system is to expect that all stakeholders are committed to its introduction. Two major change management risks often arise with PIM projects: resistance during the project, and acceptance of the PIM system after going live.

7.8.1 Resistance During the Project

We have been confronted with several reasons why a PIM system cannot be implemented or only at additional cost and time delays. Some real live examples:
- **Who is the boss**: progress is blocked because there is no agreement on who is ultimately responsible for the PIM process and its priorities. As a result the goals and direction to go cannot be fixed and the project cannot be started.
- **ICT does not feel involved**: the PIM system has been initiated by e.g. marketing together with an external supplier. ICT has not been involved in the decision-making process and actively obstructs the project by delivering corrupt data that cannot be imported.
- **No resources**: the company is already under financial pressure. Jobs have been cut and the workload is high. Management has decided to start selling online and knows this requires a PIM system. However, the additional manpower to support a PIM system is not available. No department wants to make resources available as they are already scarce.
- **Local proprietary solutions:** each country/department has already created its own desktop database, spreadsheet or paper-based PIM solution. Each solution is tailored to their specific needs and they have grown attached to it. A central PIM that saves time and resources is not a priority for them.
- **The ERP trauma:** "Not another ERP project" is an often heard fear. The company has just completed an ERP project which took years to finish and nearly brought the company to bankruptcy. However, in general, the risks with a PIM system are much lower. The project is focused on supporting one, relatively simple, process. ERP projects usually support all the main, and complex, processes of the company.

All examples are generic for the IT projects and can be solved by determining potential sources of resistance and absorbing solutions to these risks in a good project foundation with top management support.

7.8.2 Acceptance of the PIM System

People do not like to change their behavior. The same is true when people have to move away from their very efficient Excel sheets to a, in most cases, Web-based and slower PIM system. We have seen many companies follow the PIM love curve. People are initially enthusiastic about the potential benefits of PIM. However, when the system goes live, they realize that working with PIM might not be as easy as working with Excel (the Spreadsheet Paradigm is also discussed in Sect. 4.15). Only after a while do they see that they can control, maintain and distribute product information with much less effort than before (Fig. 7.4).

There are a few tricks to make sure the PIM system is accepted:
- **Burn the ships**: a Greek classic. Make sure there is no turning back. The old Excel sheets, MS Access databases and file servers should be archived as soon as all their data has been migrated to the new PIM system.

Fig. 7.4 The PIM love curve

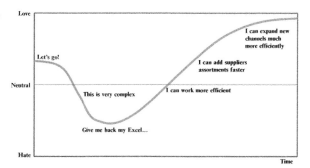

- **Training, training, training**: most companies just give one training course to their employees when the new system is introduced. The trainer is then forced to explain all the features at once. This does not work. It is better to split the course into three parts. On-board training when the system is introduced. An advanced course after 1 or 2 months to repeat the more advanced features. Finally, after 3– 6 months the really advanced features can be taught and people helped to improve how they work with the system.
- **Optimize**: the courses also allow the trainer to see where the system can be improved, based on actual usage by employees. Sometimes a few minor changes in the way the system is set up can save hours of work a day.

7.9   A PIM System Is Never Done ...

By the end of this book we believe we are far from telling you everything about PIM. However, a book has to end somewhere, and at some time you have to start making the first steps towards setting up your own PIM processes.

I believe that the opportunities and importance of PIM is going to expand significantly over the next decade and gain a position in the organization just as important as the ERP systems have today.

If you have any questions about PIM or have any experiences you would like to share, please feel free to contact me. Until then, I wish you best of luck with your PIM endeavors.

Appendix I: Cases

8

8.1 Beter Bed Holding

In bed with Product Information Management
Dirk de Bruijn, e-commerce specialist and Marisa Boselie, Product Manager

8.1.1 The Company

Beter Bed Holding operates in the European bedroom furnishings market. Its activities include retail trade through a total of 1,205 stores operating through the chains Beter Bed (the Netherlands and Belgium), Matratzen Concord (Germany, Austria, Switzerland, the Netherlands, Belgium and Poland), El Gigante del Colchón (Spain), BeddenREUS, Dormaël Slaapkamers and Slaapgenoten (all three operating in the Netherlands) and MAV (Germany). Beter Bed Holding is also involved in developing and wholesaling branded products in the bedroom furnishings sector in the Netherlands, Germany, Belgium, Spain, Austria, Switzerland and Turkey via its subsidiary DBC International. Beter Bed Holding achieved a net revenue of 397 million € in 2011.

J. Abraham, *Product Information Management*, Management for Professionals,
DOI 10.1007/978-3-319-04885-7_8, © Springer International Publishing Switzerland 2014

8.1.2   The PIM

Beter Bed decided to implement a PIM system in 2010. The key reason to improve the PIM process was the choice made by the board of Beter Bed Holding to start selling online, starting with Beter Bed in the Netherlands, followed by Matratzen Concord in Germany. Improving the PIM processes was seen as a "must have" if the new Web shop was going to work. The Board felt that only with extensive product information and photo material, would the customer experience be sufficient for consumers to order bedsteads and mattresses online. A separate PIM system was chosen for maintaining the data as the information could not easily be maintained in the existing (SAP) ERP system.

Beter Bed never considered developing a PIM system themselves. Selecting the PIM system was part of the selection procedure of the e-commerce platform. Seven systems were compared, based on several criteria about the company, functionalities, technique, costs, and implementation partners. The decision-making unit consisted of members of the ICT department, e-commerce and senior management. hybris was selected as e-commerce platform, including the hybris-PIM. The strength of the hybris PIM-module was an imported argument for this decision. After a 5 month development period, the PIM and e-commerce solution was launched for the first Web site: BeterBed.nl.

8.1.3   Product Enrichment

All products were first created in the ERP system (in the case of Beter Bed, SAP). From SAP they were exported to the PIM system where they were enriched. To improve the efficiency of the product enrichment process, the 50+ suppliers supply the product information to Beter Bed via Excel which the product data team at Beter Bed import into hybris. Beter Bed was working in this way before the PIM implementation, but the PIM requires some changes in this process which currently being implemented.

Beter Bed now manages 2,900 SKUs in the PIM system. Five-hundred new articles are added every year, and 300 are archived. While this does not sound a lot, Beter Bed made considerable effort to determine and enter all the desired product information. The goal was to give the customer an online experience at least equal to that in its stores.

As part of its strategy to provide excellent product information the number of attributes collected can be considered huge. Some examples:
- For boxsprings, not only typical attributes like product name, sizes, weight class and number of comfort zones were entered, but also information about the color and material of the feet and structure of the core.
- Likewise, for mattresses the number of feathers per m^2, the number of turns in the springs and if the mattress has handles or not.

Beter Bed also invested as much in product photography. Each bedstead and boxspring was set up and photographed. If a bedstead had multiple color variants, each color variant sold online was also photographed, meaning the same model of bedstead might have to be set up eight times for eight different colors. The same decision was made for duvet covers and other products.

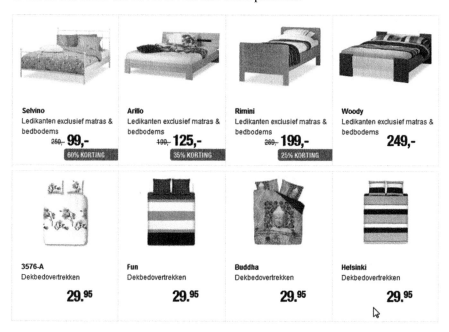

A special kind of product attribute was introduced with Unique Buying Reasons (UBRs). Examples of UBRs can be assortment or category generic such as "free shipping", "free assembly", or product specific "includes upholstered mattress" and "suitable for all seasons".

8.1.4 The Package Deal and Product Advisor

Based on the PIM system, two special online tools are offered on Beter Bed. The first is the package deal. The package deal allows customers to create their own combination of a bedstead with a frame and mattress.

Deze set samenstellen aan de hand van uw wensen ⓘ

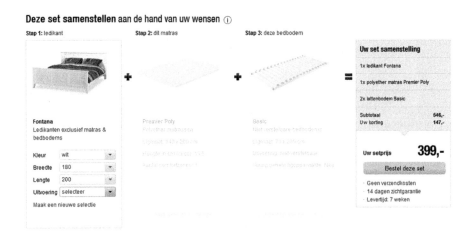

A second tool based on the PIM system, was the advisory wizard. The tool allows Beter Bed to create its own product advisors.

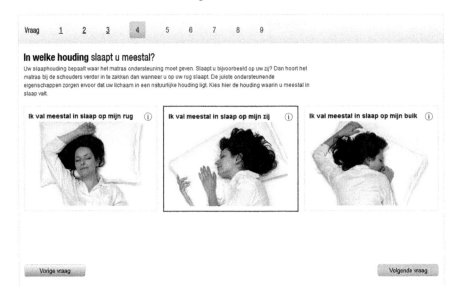

8.1.5   The Organization

The responsibility of the PIM process is spread across different departments of the organization. However, the functional owner of the application is the e-commerce specialist. Assortment maintenance, part of the purchasing department, enters and maintains all product information. Purchasing determines the assortment maintained in the PIM system, while ICT is responsible for the technical part and provides hands-on support (mass-uploads and error analysis, etc.). The different departments meet on a weekly basis to discuss progress and priorities.

8.1.6 Lessons Learned

Beter Bed learned several lessons. During the implementation phase the development of the product data model took much longer than expected. The specific product knowledge of the staff at Beter Bed had to be transferred to the implementation partner, while knowledge about the features of the PIM system had to be handed over from the implementation partner to Beter Bed.

In addition, Beter Bed had underestimated the time needed to collect and enter all product data. Dirk de Bruijn states: "Looking back, we are very proud of the results. Our Web site looks great and we are able to give the customer a much better experience than our competitors. But it was a hell of a job."

A year after going live, using the PIM system is still considered something of a challenge. Not all features are yet known to all and it proves difficult to create an overview of the entire product data model. More time should have been invested in training. The team should not only have been trained when the system was introduced, but also after the system became operational.

8.1.7 The Next Step

Beter Bed is currently developing the PIM system and Web site for its Matratzen Concord brand. The original assumption was that Beter Bed and Matratzen Concord would use the same PIM Catalog. At a superficial glance, both companies sell a comparable assortment.

However, after careful analysis, the decision was taken to set up a separate catalog for Matratzen Concord. While the hybris platform is used, the two PIM systems are separate from each other. The key reasons for this choice were, among others:
– The assortments proved to have far less overlap than originally thought;
– The preferred ways of categorizing, classifying and taking product photos differ.

With the experience gained from BeterBed.nl, and the platform for Matratzen Concord going live in October 2012, Beter Bed Holding has created a base to sell its sleeping comfort products on a European scale.

8.2 Department Store De Bijenkorf

Adding 20,000 new products, every season
Mark Mansier, Project Manager

8.2.1 The Company

De Bijenkorf is the premium department store in the Netherlands with a 140 year heritage. De Bijenkorf is known for its vast assortment of products, exceptional display windows, and special events.

At de Bijenkorf you will find top fashion, designer brands and luxury products. 4,000 employees are involved in the sale of the best products: from top brand cosmetics to the latest fashion and accessories, from tableware and toys to delicious bakery goods. De Bijenkorf is all about inspiration and experience.

De Bijenkorf has 12 branches in all large Dutch cities, with flagship stores in Amsterdam, Rotterdam and The Hague. The De Bijenkorf Web site is one of the most successful online shops in the Netherlands. In 2011 and 2012 de Bijenkorf won the ING Bricks and Clicks retail award.

8.2.2 About the PIM System

The PIM system was selected in 2009 to support the multichannel strategy of de Bijenkorf. Mark Mansier, e-commerce Business Consultant at de Bijenkorf explains: "Products and brands are core to de Bijenkorf. Almost our entire assortment is changed every year. We now have over 40,000 products with 110,000 variants in the PIM system and every season we add at least 20,000 new products. For special events like the 'Drie Dwaze Dagen' (*three crazy days*) alone we add 4,000 articles with 10,000 variants. This growth rate would have been impossible without a dedicated system to manage product information."

The PIM system gets its master data (price, stock) from Virgo, the custom, in-house developed ERP system. Also the basic product data from concessionaires, around 25 at the moment, are initially fed via Virgo to the PIM system. Further enrichment is done in the PIM system. The number of attributes added differs strongly per product category. For T-shirts this is approximately 5–7 attributes. For electronics this may be more than 30.

As one of the multi-channel frontrunners in the Netherlands, the PIM system has several channels to which it delivers its product data among which the Web shop (http://www.bijenkorf.nl), a responsive design site (m.bijenkorf.nl) for mobile traffic, and apps for the iPhone, iPad, and Android.

After initial implementation, de Bijenkorf has continued to invest in improving the PIM processes and the PIM system. Concessionaires provide their article information, which is imported into Virgo. Virgo exports CSV files which are imported into the PIM system. The quality of these data feeds can however sometimes be poor. De Bijenkorf therefore also adapted its purchasing contracts to make sure the supplier is responsible for the prices he provides. To be on the safe side, de Bijenkorf also built in more data validations and control mechanisms to prevent erroneous data from ever reaching the consumer.

Improvements include:

- customized search queries to search for partly-enriched products, products not assigned to a category, SKUs not assigned to a product, etc.;
- optimize processes to reduce the workload e.g. enriching articles automatically, adding promotion codes straight to products, assigning products automatically to the photo studio, etc.;
- enrichment of each product detail page via the PIM system for SEO purposes.

The PIM system is also used to support more complex product structures like product bundles and cross selling these bundles. As MAM system two simple file servers are used to store all photos and video material.

8.2.3   The PIM Organization

The e-commerce department at de Bijenkorf is responsible for the PIM system. The department is divided into several teams. Two teams have been set up for product information:

- Enrichment team: This team is based at Docdata, the warehouse and distribution partner of de Bijenkorf. As the assortment of de Bijenkorf is strongly season based, the work is highly seasonal with high peaks. On average 2 people work full time for de Bijenkorf. Three can be added during peaks. Each team member enriches 50 products per day including photos. When a new assortment arrives, a pick batch is created and the regular articles are sent to the Docdata photo studio (luxury items are photographed by a third party—Lukkien). Multiple photos are made per product and in some cases also video. Attribute information is added by the team. Guidelines have been set up on how to write for different product categories considering what customers want to know, and for search engine optimization.
- Assortment team: This team of approximately 12 people is based at the headquarters of de Bijenkorf. A team of 2 (an assortment specialist and an assistant) are responsible for a specific product category. The assortment is determined by this team in close cooperation with purchasing. The team also validates the work of the enrichment team and publishes the products. During special sales periods, like the famous "Drie Dwaze Dagen" temporary staff join the team.

Other teams in the e-commerce department are Business Development (business and functional analysts and project managers, an in-house front-end developer and an e-commerce IT-architect, seven FTE total), Online Marketing (a marketeer, SEO expert and SEA expert), Content and Design (who manage all non-product related content including marketing campaigns, eight FTE) and Operations (a manager, two operations coordinators, two assistants and a customer care coordinator for 2nd and 3rd line questions). The customer care team is partly located in-house and partly outsourced to manage peaks in calls and email traffic.

8.2.4   Creating a Product Data Model

Setting up and maintaining the product data model has proven complex. Most products in Virgo do not have an EAN code. Instead each article in Virgo is given a custom article code based on the following coding mechanism:
- The first four digits are based on the reporting group (e.g. Women's fashion, Toys, Accessories);
- The fifth digit is the kind of product. This is no longer actively used and is usually "0";
- The sixth digit is the season number. There are one to eight seasons (covering 2 years). Number "9" represents products that are never out of stock and are not season bound.
- The seventh through tenth digits represent the product code, e.g. "1234" of "7812".
- The 11th and 12th digits represent the product color;
- Finally, the last three digits represent the sizes of the different variants where "000" means there is no size variant.

There were some challenges with this coding mechanism. For example, after going through eight seasons, the same product code is used again for a different product. However, customers may like to see what they bought several years ago. Technically this issue could be solved in the PIM by allowing one season to be stored twice in the PIM system.

Creating a data model in the PIM system that solves these limitations of the ERP system, and several other related issues, required very strong abstract thinking skills. The data model was therefore first maintained by the Business Development team.

8.2.5   PIM Benefits

Fashion labels, designer brands and luxury products are core to the proposition of de Bijenkorf. Presenting brand products in the right way via all channels is therefore crucial. Adding more photos (from three to five), video and specific size tables has improved the customer experience and reduced the return ratio. The PIM system is now also used to store information about the sizes of the model showing the products. Everything is done to enhance the customer experience.

In addition, the PIM system enriches management reports with information about how often a product is viewed, how many products in a category are sold, etc. The product photos are also used to make the reporting dashboards more visual.

8.2.6   The Future

PIM is becoming an increasingly important process touching increasing numbers of departments at de Bijenkorf. While Purchasing focused in the past mainly on buying products, they are increasingly becoming part of the PIM process. When entering new products in Virgo, several details have already to be entered in order to sell the product (e.g. sleeve size and collar size).

The technical features of the PIM system have proven more extensive with regard to product information than the current ERP system. De Bijenkorf is therefore considering turning the process around. Products are first entered in the PIM system. Only when sold are they added on the fly to the ERP system. This change may even be required as de Bijenkorf plans to expand its concessionaires from 25 to 35 in the coming year. Adding long-tail assortment first in the ERP system would pollute the system with products that are never sold and may reduce its technical performance.

8.3   PIM @ Coca-Cola HBC Schweiz AG

Using PIM for a Better Customer Experience
Roman Desponds, eBusiness specialist and Mathis Fluck, Project Leader

8.3.1   The Company

Coca-Cola HBC Switzerland is one of the largest companies in the non-alcoholic beverage industry in the country and is a franchised bottler of The Coca-Cola Company. With 1,000 employees the company serves approximately 60,000 customers. Coca-Cola HBC Switzerland produces, sells and distributes both leading brands such as Coca-Cola, Coca-Cola light (diet Coke), Fanta and Sprite, local brands such as Valser and brands licensed by other companies, such as Nestea.

8.3.2   Why PIM?

The key reason for Coca-Cola HBC to select a PIM system was the replacement of their old Web site in 2010 with a new e-commerce platform. The number of products managed by the company is actually quite low (300, with 50 new products added each year in two languages, French and German). However, for the new e-commerce platform is was felt key to provide better and more extensive product information. With the earlier system there were several product content quality issues which needed to be resolved. In addition, Coca-Cola HBC was looking for a system that was able to manage different assortments and prices for each customer segment and key account—features that the ERP system could at that time not support.

The eBusiness Unit, which is part of the Customer Service Center department, is responsible for the PIM system. The master data is provided by the ERP system. The marketing department provides all the enriched product data, already translated in a text file. This information is re-entered by the eBusiness unit into the PIM system.

The PIM system distributes the information to the company's ten different Web shops including two B2B shops for the normal assortment of the company, an employee shop where staff can buy products at a discount, a B2B loyalty shop with merchandise products and several customized Web shops developed for large accounts of the bottler company. All media assets (photos, pack shots and videos) are maintained in a separate system, NC AG Switzerland.

A complex product data structure was needed to support the calculation of logistical conditions (e.g. weights, sizes, number of products per SKU type (sku, layer, pallet), etc.). Conversion rules are also used, e.g. to translate hectoliters into liters.

The product lifecycle is managed in a simpler fashion. New products are automatically transferred from the ERP system to the PIM system, added to the assortment and manually enlarged with data in the PIM system. Old products or out of stock products are set automatically to inactive.

8.3.3   PIM Benefits

Selling the Web shop and PIM to management was not easy. The management strongly believed in personal selling and was dubious as to whether customers would use the online ordering facility. However, in the end, the project was approved.

The PIM has proven to be of strategic value to Coca-Cola HBC. It allows the company to add within 2 weeks a new Web shop with a specific design, assortment and prices for a key account. Not only Coca-Cola specific assortment can be added but also third party products. This allows the company to deliver extra value to its customers as they can use one portal to order many different beverage products from several suppliers.

In addition to the strategic benefits, tactical and operational benefits have also been realized. Mr. Roman Desponds, eBusiness specialist at Coca-Cola HBC Switzerland states: "The actual PIM system allows us to reduce the costs of our classical offline order channels."

On a tactical level, Coca-Cola HBC is much better able to control assortments, prices and product content per supplier. On an operational level, Coca-Cola HBC has been able to realize cost reductions as the new system is easier to use, reducing the amount of training needed and allowing people to enter content faster. Turnover has also increased thanks to the new Web shop. About 50 % of the customer base are now using the online platform and online customers are ordering 7 % more (both more kinds of products and more of the same products) than via fax or email.

Other benefits include further professionalization of the order process and significant reductions in the number of errors in this process.

8.3.4 Looking Back and Forward

Project implementation was more complex than originally thought. Especially connecting the ERP system to the PIM system and creating the product data model took more time. Planned weekly meetings with the implementation agency (both the project leader and product data specialist) and IT representatives and project team members from Coca-Cola HBC helped to resolve these challenges.

Internally the new PIM and e-commerce systems were welcomed, but externally some customers were less keen on new technologies and having to change their behavior. This was however resolved through training courses and argument lists for the customer service center.

Looking forward, the PIM and e-commerce system at Coca-Cola HBC has attracted international attention. Coca-Cola HBC is planning to roll out the system to several other countries. In Switzerland the number of products as well as key account Web sites will be steadily expanded.

8.4 CRH Construction Materials

Using the long tail as strategic advantage
Kees Heddes, PIM Manager

8.4.1 The Company

CRH is an international leader in building materials. The company is a diversified building materials group that manufactures and distributes building material products from the fundamentals of heavy materials and elements to construct the frame, through value-added exterior products that complete the building envelope, to distribution channels that service construction fit-out and renewal. CRH employs approximately 76,000 people at 3,600 operating locations in 34 countries.

CRH Bouwmaterialen is the Dutch division of CRH and market leader in construction material in the Netherlands. The company has over 80 branches under several local and national brand names: Bakker Nijboer, BBN, DeBoo, Erven Feenstra, BMN, Stoel Van Klaveren, Timo.nl, Van Neerbos, Wijck's and NVB Ubbens (Fig. 8.1).

8.4.2 Why PIM?

The key reason for CRH to start a PIM project in January 2012 was the decision to build a B2B and B2C e-commerce platform. PIM went live in July 2012 and at the moment (November 2012) already offers 152,000 products.

Fig. 8.1 CRH products are sold per item, pallet or truck

The plan is to let the PIM grow quickly over the next few years by importing entire assortments from suppliers. The aim is to grow to three million products in 2015.

8.4.3   About the PIM System

The PIM system receives data from three different sources. An external data provider delivers the base and partly enriched product data. The CRH ERP system delivers price and stock levels. Finally, ETIM is used as the base for the classification model. Media assets are maintained directly in PIM, in this case hybris.

CRH opted for ETIM as the base for its classification model as it allowed for a free and quick start in building the product data model. The Product Assortment Management department maintains the product data model and enriches ETIM with classification classes for building materials. The department is also responsible for enriching the attributes with additional information. This, for example, allows the user to see information about a facet on the Web site.

The product data model has been given to the external data provider who enriches the product information in line with the wishes of CRH. The external provider gathers information from 116 suppliers. The number of suppliers is expected to grow to 240 in 2013. The external data provider delivers approximately 80 % of the desired information (about 35 attributes are collected per product including photos, videos and gross prices).

After external enrichment, the product data is imported into the PIM system. The Content Management department validates the quality of the product data provided and enriches it further where necessary.

The sales department sorts the products into a commercial product categorization. This is done twice, once for the B2B Web site and once for the B2C Web site (called Timo.nl). As an ERP categorization tree is also imported from the ERP system, this actually involved mapping ERP product categories to Web categories and it can therefore be done in a reasonable amount of time.

The Purchasing department has ultimate responsibility for the PIM and the PIM Manager, Kees Heddes, coordinates the different priorities of the departments and oversees the entire process.

The PIM system is used to support several complex data structures. Easy relationships (cross-sell, up-sell, accessories and replacement products) are maintained in the ERP system and exported to the PIM system. However, unit management is done in the PIM system. Here again ETIM is used as base for conversions (e.g. 1,000 grams is 1 kilo and 1,000 kilos is one ton).

8.4.4   PIM Benefits

The PIM system has proven to be a strategic asset for CRH. It allows the company to sell the entire assortments of its suppliers to its customers. This results in additional turnover with its existing customers and allows the company to gain new customers interested in the one-stop shopping service CRH is now able to deliver.

The system is also used as a knowledge base for its employees who can look up products much more easily and filter down to the specific product that best meets the needs of their customers.

On an operational level, it has allowed CRH to kick start its e-commerce initiative in an efficient way. The PIM system now allows CRH to efficiently manage tens of thousands of products. In the future the PIM system will support the automatic import of supplier data from over 700 suppliers and an offering of more than three million products.

8.4.5   Implementing the PIM

One of the main challenges during PIM implementation proved to be the product data model. Understanding and creating a sound data model in close cooperation with internal departments like Sales, e-commerce, the external data provider and the implementation partner turned out to be more complex and to take longer than expected.

In addition, management expectations were very high regarding the speed with which products could be imported and enriched. It took more time and effort to increase the assortment while keeping the data quality at the necessary high level.

There was some resistance from the Content Management department regarding the PIM as most of the work would have to be done by this unit. However, by announcing the implementation more than 2 years in advance and involving them in the process, the change was accepted.

8.4.6 Looking Forward

A PIM is never finished. Several processes can be improved and further optimized, such as the process of getting the data back from the data provider. This process still involves several manual tasks that could be automated.

A larger concern is data quality control. It is currently not possible to compare new supplier data with previous data. CRH wishes to see changes made by suppliers first on a global view and then to be able to zoom in on product and attribute level. More and better functionality is needed to keep an overview of what was changed by suppliers.

An third serious concern is that the product cockpit of the PIM is too slow to maintain the large number of products. Response times are too long. The technical partner is currently looking for ways to improve this.

Other wishes for 2013 include improving the mass edit features in the PIM system (now product information has to be changed record by record) and to connect the PIM system to the new ERP system which will go live end 2013.

Businesswise, CRH also has several goals for 2013 and beyond. Apart from a further implementation of the long-tail strategy, CRH aims for 99 % of all product information to be fed from the PIM into the ERP system in the future. Likewise, the number of Web sites that use the PIM system will be expanded.

8.5   Fabory Group

10 years PIM experience
Angelique Vervloet, Manager Product Information/Peter Beekmans, Database Administrator

8.5.1 The Company

Fabory Group, founded in 1947, is an international group of leading technical business enterprises with more than 140 locations in 15 countries and a strong team of 1,700 fastener experts. High quality fastening materials and systems are marketed worldwide under the Fabory brand. In addition, a range of A-brand tools and industrial supplies are offered to support the fastener range. In total Fabory offers more than 50,000 different fasteners, 30,000 tools 10,000 industrial supplies and 6,000 safety products.

8.5.2 A Long PIM History

As a wholesaler of fasteners, Fabory has a long product information management history. In the 1990s, Fabory was already using a PIM system to create a printed catalog. However, this PIM system had to be replaced as it could not export its data efficiently to Fabory's Web site. The new system, called Fabory Catalog System (FCS), also has a long track record. Fabory eventually chose to custom develop its PIM system. Development was initiated in January 2002 and the system went live in July 2004. The first catalog was printed in January 2005.

FCS contains 91,000 SKUs in more than 3,000 product categories. On average between 15 and 20 attributes are maintained for each SKU. 10,000 articles are added every year and 2,000 are archived. Product information is fully maintained in nine languages: Dutch, French, English, Portuguese, Czech, Polish, Romanian, and partly in three languages: Bulgarian, German and Spanish. The translations are done by the local Fabory sales offices and occasionally by translation agencies. The Master Data is retrieved from Fabory's SAP system and the PIM system distributes the enriched product data to several channels among which Framemaker, to create the print catalog, and hybris, the e-commerce platform of Fabory.

Fabory has created several catalogs in the PIM system. For print, four catalogs have been set up (for tools, fasteners, tool suppliers and own sales organization) and an online catalog is available for each sales organization. Fabory also uses several categorizations. The ERP category tree is supported and two new categorizations have been introduced: one for print, and one for online. This was done because Fabory discovered that products have to be sorted differently in a print catalog (based on alphabet) than online (based on popularity). In addition, Fabory's PIM system supports several classification classes such as UNSPSC, ETIM, ICS, ECLASS which are preferred by their customers.

8.5.3 The Organization

The Marketing Department has ultimate responsibility for the PIM system. Marketing does most of the product enrichment and collects all photo and media assets. Several departments use the information among which are product category management (for the creation of the print catalog), eBusiness (for the Web site) and Product Information Management (for the link with the ERP system and for managing all master data). A separate PIM manager has been assigned to manage the wishes and priorities of the various departments.

8.5.4 PIM Benefits

Fabory has remained a strong believer in PIM over the last decade. Angelique Vervloet says: "Fabory has a long-standing reputation for reliable data when it comes to fasteners. Because our assortment includes different brands, the specifications we receive from suppliers are very different. We aim to standardize the content so that customers can find products more easily and we need to be aware of the fact that details do make a difference."

The PIM system has not only proven an enabler of Fabory's long-tail strategy, it has also improved the experience customers have with Fabory as a fastening specialist. On a tactical level, it allows Fabory to distribute its content in a controlled way towards its sales organizations and customers. On an operational level, it has enabled Fabory to sell highly specialized products online.

8.5.5   The Future

Fabory is currently looking to replace FCS. The PIM system is increasingly becoming a central system in Fabory. Several features, such as importing supplier data, creating BMECAT files and maintenance of the classification structure are today covered by standard PIM systems but are not supported by FCS. And the company that custom developed FCS no longer exists. Fabory management has therefore decided to enter the next decade with a new PIM system.

8.6   Manor

Continuously improving PIM processes
  Alain Stopnicer, Head of Operations e-Manor

8.6.1   The Company

With 60 % market share, Manor is Switzerland's leading Department Store chain. Manor's history begins at the end of the nineteenth century. In 1902, three businessmen opened the "Léon Nordmann" department store on the Weggisgasse in Lucerne. It is considered the origin of what Manor is today. The company name Manor was first used in 1965 when a new corporate identity was created. Since 1994, all company stores in German-speaking Switzerland have been renamed Manor. In 2000 all stores carry the Manor name.

Its slogan '*donnons du style à la vie*' stands for great style at affordable prices. With 65 department stores, CHF 2.87 billion turnover and around 11,000 employees in 2011 Manor is the biggest retailer in Perfumery and Home Accessories in Switzerland and the number two in Fashion.

8.6.2   Why a PIM System?

In November 2009 Manor decided to develop a new Web shop. Manor offers more than 200,000 SKUs online of which 140,000 fashion related items are changed annually. Online, the assortment is expected to grow by 50,000 items per year. A specialized PIM system is therefore deemed essential. The existing ERP system is not thought to be very user-friendly and does not support several key PIM processes. It is believed that it is easier and faster to buy an external system instead of custom building PIM functionality into the custom ERP system.

8.6.3 About the PIM System

The new PIM system went live in August 2010. Base information i.e. prices and stock levels, are interfaced from Manor's ERP system and logistical partner system. Products are declared "online products" in ERP by the Buying Department. A product is taken off the Web shop automatically when product availability in the ERP system reaches zero or the product is tagged as being removed from the assortment. For exceptional cases, the online merchandiser can change the status of a product to inactive directly in the PIM system.

The level of product enrichment differs widely per product category. Fashion products may only have five attributes. For multimedia items this may be up to 20 or more. The product information is maintained in the three most used languages in Switzerland: German, French and Italian. All photo material is maintained in a third party MAM system (Celum).

Apart from the Web site, the PIM system is also used for in-store product descriptions on displays, even for departments, whose assortment is not offered on the Internet (e.g. Multimedia).

8.6.4 The PIM Organization

The e-commerce unit is ultimately responsible for the PIM system. However, several departments are part of the PIM process, and the process differs widely from department to department. The Food & Wine and Multimedia departments enter their product data directly into the PIM system: The Multimedia department needs the data anyway for the product descriptions in-store and the Food & Wine department needs the information to make a degustation of all wines to get proper, comparable degustation notes. But these are exceptions. If not necessary (for know-how or in-store reasons), the Purchasing Department is not involved and the e-commerce Department takes care of the product information process. For instance, the Beauty and Fashion units depend on the e-commerce unit for data entry.

There are three different PIM roles in the e-commerce department:
- Gathering data: several people make sure that all the information needed is collected. If necessary suppliers are contacted for additional information. Mr. Stopnicer, Head of Operations at e-Manor comments: "Getting information from suppliers has proved to be a disappointment. The quality of the data and level of automation differs strongly across suppliers. Some still send printed

information, some CDs, some have download-links and some don't even have any product information at all. No standard can be applied. You start with every supplier from scratch." This process is improving slowly. The first the top five suppliers in each category are identified and a solution is sought that fits these suppliers. Based on the solution, Manor tries to convince smaller suppliers to use the same approach.

- Entering data: several people are employed to enter product data from known sources into the PIM system, or to verify whether imported data is correct. Data quality is still a major issue, and commercial texts in particular require validation.
- Translation: the base data is entered in German. French and Italian translations are done by external agencies and returned to Manor. They are entered manually in the PIM system by the data entry team.
- Merchandising: five online merchandisers are the key contact with the Purchasing Department. Together they determine which products are sold online. The merchandisers assign products to Web categories, do a final quality check and publish the products to the production environment. They also supervise the automatic replenishment parameters and change them immediately if necessary.

8.6.5   Selecting the PIM

To realize its e-commerce strategy Manor understood from the start that a PIM system was needed. The company defined several use-cases (functional specifications) which the software vendor had to show during live demos with real data. The language issue was particularly important. All PIMs claim to work in multi languages, but in the case of Manor one person enters all languages for one product. There are no teams/people per language.

Mr. Stopnicer states: "Checking the most important, and time-consuming, use-cases with the people doing this job on a daily basis was definitely an excellent choice. By involving future users who would be entering the data into the PIM system, the final choice for the PIM system soon gained very high credibility and commitment."

hybris was ultimately selected as the software vendor because they offered both an e-commerce and a PIM solution and its PIM module best fitted the predefined user stories.

8.6.6   Implementing the PIM System

Manor's main challenge during implementation proved to be the product data model. The Web categories were completely different from the category tree used in the ERP system. Fashion has products and variants (where different colors can even have different prices), whereas in the wine business a product equals one variant.

The e-commerce Merchandiser and the Purchasing Department were involved to define which attributes were needed, and the potential information sources. Then IT was involved to establish which information already existed in ERP and checked whether the data quality was high enough to also be used online.

Not surprisingly, information was available in the ERP system but in the end never used as the quality was generally poor: some fields were used by the Purchasing Department to keep notes on products, no general rules existed for product descriptions and typing and spelling errors were commonplace.

A second challenge proved to be product data entry and training. Not only was data entry itself far more time consuming than initially thought, training people to enter data correctly and spread the know-how on product structures and processes also took time. The investment in training and education paid off. In general, users working with the PIM system give more detailed and better feedback and bug descriptions, and have more patience with change requests now that they have an idea about the complexity of the whole system.

8.6.7 Looking Forward

Manor still has several PIM processes they want to improve. On a strategic level Manor hopes to continue to expand the number of online categories (home, bath, etc.). To do this Manor will also review its existing photo and content creation process. For example, make the existing functional product descriptions more graphical and easier-to-read for the POS.

Improvements are also being implemented on an operational level. For example, translations are currently entered manually into the PIM system. This process is considered too shaky and slow. A project has been set up to give translation agencies direct access (via an interface) to the product data that requires translation.

Similarly, some use-cases like analytics/reporting/alerting were not specified fully up front. As a result, workflow and reports to improve the quality of the product information are missing. However, these insights are essential in order to get a better overview of which data is missing and to get products online. This functionality will also be added in the near future.

Mr. Stopnicer comments: "We have made our first steps with the new PIM system. We are however discovering that we can improve our processes all the time. With the number of products and number of users growing, we will keep on investing in expanding and optimizing our PIM system."

8.7 Nikon Europe

Creating a governance model for PIM
Laurent Christen, Head of Direct Sales

8.7.1 The Company

Nikon is well known as market leader in imaging products, and its technologies continue to play a significant role in defining the photographic industry. Nikon offers photographic products for both consumers and the professional market.

8.7.2 Why a PIM?

In 2010 Nikon Europe initiated an e-commerce strategy to serve both consumers, its network of wholesalers and retailers, and own employees online. hybris was selected as e-commerce and PIM system.

A PIM system was considered an essential part of the e-commerce strategy. Mr. Christen, head of direct sales for Nikon Europe explains: "Nikon is a product manufacturer. Product information, technical specifications, images, etc. They are the bread and butter of our company. Without a PIM we don't sell anything. The lifecycle of a product has to be managed from idea to end of life. It's not a question of why. It is a must have."

8.7.3 About the PIM

Currently some 1,300 active SKUs are maintained in the PIM system including 800 cameras and 500 accessories. However, 8,000 end of life products were also added to the PIM system to up to 8 years ago.

On average 20 attributes are stored per product for external use. In addition, 30+ attributes are added for internal use. The PIM system is also used to create relationships between products. For example for cross selling purposes or to communicate which products are accessories of the base product, like batteries.

Another example where product relationships are created is for compatibility where one product may be compatible (or serve as replacement part) for several other products.

Mediabin from Interwoven is used as worldwide Media Asset Management system. All the above line product information (product images in high resolution, videos, 360, TV commercials, etc.) are stored in Mediabin. All media assets are imported into hybris.

Sometimes relationships can be complex. A product, for example a lens, can be sold as part of a child product of a base product, as a standalone product or be part of a specially created marketing bundle.

In the past each country maintained its own system to manage relationships or create bundles. All relationships are now managed centrally and marketing bundles are likewise created increasingly on a European level as the Internet is becoming the main communication channel.

The information from the PIM system is used across almost all possible channels: TV adds, radio, banners, commercials, flyers and of course the Nikon e-commerce platform. Several sites have been set up within the e-commerce platform to serve consumers, wholesales/retailers, local sales organizations and employees.

8.7.4 The PIM Process

Approximately 80 new products are added every year. This process starts when the decision has been made to manufacture a product, which is usually 1 year prior to the actual sales launch. First a unique product development product ID is created in Japan in the company's ERP system, SAP. This code is only used for internal communication.

To prevent a product from being shown via any of Nikon's Web sites before the World Wide Announcement (WWA), for every product published an automatic check is done in real time to check with the corporate Web site built on Interwoven whether publication is allowed.

When the product becomes available in SAP, this is the starting point for enrichment of the product by the different regions (Europe, Americas, China, Asia-Pacific and Japan). Nikon Europe product enrichment tasks include adding a uniform product name, product descriptions, commercial product attributes and mapping the photos to specific products. Technical specifications have also to be normalized as multiple names are used in the SAP system for the same unit (for example for pixels, also pxl, pix, mpixels are used) and values are not standardized (e.g. white is also described as W or WH).

As Nikon Europe sells in 35 European countries, localization is key. Nikon Europe enriches the base information in English and then uses several translation agencies such as Translation.com and Linebridge to translate all the information into dozens of different languages.

A separate PIM catalog is created for each of the 35 countries based on the master data. Each country has its own prices, promotions and assortment and may support multiple languages. As products are sometimes launched while the translation process is not yet finished, an extensive fall-back system has been set up in the PIM system. For example, if the French version for Switzerland is not yet available, the system falls back on French—French. Only if no information is available in this language/country combination, is UK English shown.

A glossary is maintained centrally to make sure that the translation per country is done the same way in a country each time. For example, the term flashlight may be named speed light, flashgun or flashes in different English speaking countries.

The e-commerce team checks the translation first and following approval it is sent to subject matter experts (SME) who are native speakers. The SME is usually a person in the local sales organization, a local freelancer or local media agency. As they know the products well, they can validate the translations best. The SME gives feedback to the translation agency and may add new terms to the glossary. After the SME approves the translation, the information is released for publication.

8.7.5   The PIM Organization

All departments at Nikon Europe (marketing, logistics, sales, local sales offices, finance, e-commerce) use the PIM system to some extent. In addition (local) media agencies either add or consume content.

Before 2010 each department had its own way of collecting and distributing product data. The existing models in these departments were, to some extent, copied into the new PIM system. Each department maintains its own data in the system. As there are overlaps, this sometimes results in data changes in one department impacting data from other departments in a negative way.

There is currently not yet a formal owner for the PIM process and system. The management focus was on building the e-commerce platform and the importance of implementing a well-structured PIM process was underestimated. However, it became clear with the introduction of the e-commerce system, that a lot of information was not entered correctly or was not standardized.

As key user, the e-commerce department has taken the lead in improving the PIM process. The e-commerce department started pushing towards a uniform data model and took the lead in determining which data is maintained and where.

There were several challenges surrounding the data model. In the central DAM system and corporate Web site all the different colors of the Nikon 1 are stored as one product. However, in the SAP system (and PIM) the products are seen as one base product with multiple variants. As a result, product information and photo material from the central DAM system and corporate Web site have to be mapped manually to the data coming out of the SAP system.

To improve the process, the e-commerce department is very strict in not changing data in a system if that system is not the master. By not making it possible to fix data in a local system, the creation of (new) data islands are prevented.

8.7.6   Looking Forward

The PIM system has been like a mirror for Nikon. Mr. Christen explains: "As consumers see more or our data, you get more feedback on how to improve data. Nikon is continuously improving data because the data is exposed to the consumer. Our organization is increasingly aware that they have to enter and use correct, consumer friendly product data. But this requires us to change our behavior and the way we have acted for 10 years or more."

Nikon has started with low quality product data. Over the last 2 years the data quality has improved significantly with the effort put in by several individuals and departments. There is now more support to create a central master data management strategy, formalize the processes and set up a clear governance model. This process could not have started earlier as the organization was not yet convinced of the importance of good product data. A bottom-up approach was needed to prove the worth of this. Nikon is now ready to start a top-down project.

8.8   PVG

Implementing a cross border PIM system
   Gijs   van   Wanrooy,   Marketing   Manager/Loes   Kamerman,   Marketing-communication

8.8.1   The Organization

The PVG Group, an international trading house, has over 30 years' experience in the purchase, marketing, distribution and sale of a wide range of products in the air treatment field. Via its own A-brand Zibro, PVG is focused on improving the climate in the personal living environment. The PVG Group has 160 employees generating a turnover of around 180 million €. In its business operations, PVG upholds the principle "Think global, act local". PVG commercializes its products in 14 European countries with the help of 7 local offices and 13,000 resellers.

8.8.2 Creating a PIM Business Case

It took a long time for PVG's management to make the decision to implement a PIM system. The discussions about improving PIM processes started in 2006. It was however not considered top priority. It therefore took until 2009 before the decision was made to invest in a PIM system.

The change of heart was caused by two developments. Due to the financial crisis, the company needed restructuring, and increasing efficiency became a top priority. Management saw a PIM system as one of the possible solutions to pursue this objective.

A second factor was the decision to start selling the Zibro products online, B2B. This was part of an overall strategy to make the most of PVG's product information available online for all its customer groups.

8.8.3   Sources and Channels

The PIM system maintains 4,000 SKUs, both base products and spare parts. Around 250–300 new SKUs are added every year (7 %). In addition, information about old products are continuously added to the PIM system. The aim of the PIM was not only to sell new products but also to provide after-sales service for existing customers. Most of PVG's products have a product lifetime of 25 years and PVG is asked questions about its assortment on a daily basis.

Product information is gathered from several sources. The marketing department enters the information and is responsible for a consistent up-to-date PIM system. Localization and translation of the content into six languages is done by the local offices. The initial idea was for the product development department to also use the PIM system to support the product development process. However, this concept was skipped. Some products considered never reached the sales phase and the information started to pollute instead of enrich the PIM system.

The PIM system is used intensively both internally and externally. Internally the system is used by the 7 local offices, 80 after-sales offices and 13,000 resellers of PVG products. Resellers and consumers have limited access. After-Sales has full access to all content in the PIM system. The local offices use the PIM systems in their marketing, sales support and after-sales departments to answer questions from customers quickly and efficiently. They also guide people through the system so that next time they look for information they can do it themselves e.g. commercial and technical specs, product sheets, manuals, images, and exploded views.

8.8.4   PIM Benefits

Before implementing the PIM system, information was managed centrally and locally. Headquarters provided information in English on paper or digitally and each local office translated this locally using MS Excel, Word or a proprietary database. Not supporting the PIM processes led to two main issues. The quality of the local solutions differed widely. Headquarters often received product enquiries while the information should have been available locally. In addition, when product information changes centrally, the information was often not updated locally, resulting in local offices with outdated information.

The implementation of the PIM solution allowed PVG to solve these inefficiencies. In addition, reseller and end-customer satisfaction improved. Before the PIM system was implemented PVG's after-sales offices were difficult to reach. In the peak season around 200 calls were handled every day. Gijs van Wanrooy, marketing manager at PVG, states that this number has been reduced by over 50 % thanks to the implementation of the PIM system.

In addition, the central marketing department observed that resellers are no longer contacting them for product information and photo material as the up-to-date information is available online. This allows PVG employees to focus on other tasks.

8.8.5 Organization

Gijs van Wanrooy, Marketing Manager of PVG is ultimately responsible for the PIM system. The operational responsibilities lie with Loes Kamerman who is assisted by an intern.

All data is entered in English by Gijs' team. A workflow process was defined to make sure all product information is translated by the local offices into six different languages. Now the basic structure has been set up, all data is updated centrally.

In the implementation phase, four interns were entering the data on a full-time basis for 3 months. Nowadays, since only 250 to new 300 SKUs are entered every year, an intern for 1 day a week is enough to keep the PIM system up to date.

8.8.6 Lessons Learned

Mr. van Wanrooy has learned several lessons from the implementation of the PIM system. Most apply to all major organizational changes.

For example, high quality up-to-date online product information is a must for every organization nowadays in order to communicate efficiently with all stakeholders. According to Mr. van Wanrooy, the world around us is changing very quickly. New markets, new products, consumers who change their behavior, new distribution channels, and we are confronted almost every single day with new IT solutions. If you want to stay connected, just make sure your organization also changes each year by 10 %.

Moreover, every time you implement a new IT solution, the old is, of course, always better, easier and more complete in people's minds. Therefore Mr. van Wanrooy states you have to stay focused and create with your team a new way of working more efficiently with each other. The best way of doing this in the case of a PIM system, is to only provide product information via the PIM system. It is however crucial that the information is then also completely up-to-date. If the information were not of excellent quality, the local offices would have fallen back on their own tools and systems, and other stakeholders would not use it at all.

Also knowledge transfer and training proved to be important. Generally speaking, training is something that could have been done better. Instead of providing only a basic training course at the start, it would have been better to provide additional training on the job. This would have allowed users to ask questions and would have resulted in a less steep learning curve, and in the PIM system being used optimally much sooner.

8.9 The Look/PKZ

PIM as Base for an Omnichannel Strategy
  Nicolas Schibler, Manager e-commerce

8.9.1   The Company

The fashion company PKZ Burger-Kehl & Co. AG (PKZ) was founded in 1881 by
Paul Kehl. With an annual turnover of over 200 million Swiss Francs and
700 employees, PKZ is one of the leading Swiss Fashion retailers for men's and
women's apparel in the mid to high price segment.

   PKZ owns 50 stores with the following retail brands:
- PKZ: with 35 stores PKZ is the men's fashion specialist in Switzerland.
- Feldpausch: acquired in 1997, Feldpausch leads the way in fashion for the
  independent and fashionable woman.
- Blue Dog: founded in 1994 as casual wear brand for both men and women, Blue
  Dog is sold in its own shops and by the PKZ and Feldpausch stores.
- Burger: the Burger store with over 800 m^2 was opened in 2002 in the shopping
  hotspot of Switzerland, the Bahnhofstrasse in Zurich. Burger is the place where
  young urban people can find all the trendy brands in high-end casual and design
  fashion.

8.9.2   Opting for a PIM System

Seeing that younger generations are turning to the Internet for fashion inspiration
and orientation, PKZ Management developed an omnichannel strategy where the
information and purchasing processes of their customers are supported independent
of the channels they use.

   Instead of developing four different brand shops, a decision was taken to launch
one overarching brand: The Look. The Look is both a loyalty card concept, the
largest fashion and lifestyle magazine in Switzerland (circulation 450,000) and a
multichannel inspiration and shopping platform supporting several different communication channels: Web site, mobile, and social media.

   The decision to build an omnichannel platform was made in 2010. The Look was
launched in October 2011. The PIM system is the base for the omnichannel
platform. No real PIM system was present in the company. The company's ERP
system was custom-developed based on the particular needs of the company and
contains all the master data information. However, it was not considered prudent to
expand the ERP system with more product data. Therefore the decision was taken to

set up a separate PIM system to enable the company to create the same brand and product feel online as well as offline. When hybris was selected as e-commerce system, the choice to also use the hybris PIM system was quickly made.

8.9.3 The PIM Organization

The PKZ PIM system contains between 13,000 and 15,000 SKUs. As fashion retailer, between 4,000 and 5,000 new products are introduced each season (spring/summer, autumn/winter).

The PIM unit is part of the e-commerce department and consists of two separate teams:

- A content team of four who enter all product information and translate the information from German into French.
- A photo production team of three photographers, three stylists and one team leader.

Mr. Schibler, e-commerce manager at PKZ, is also responsible for the PIM team. He states: "A large PIM team is one of the big differences between fashion and for example wholesale companies. Fashion retailers have to create all their product information themselves, while wholesalers have to focus on gathering product information."

8.9.4 Product Enrichment and Look

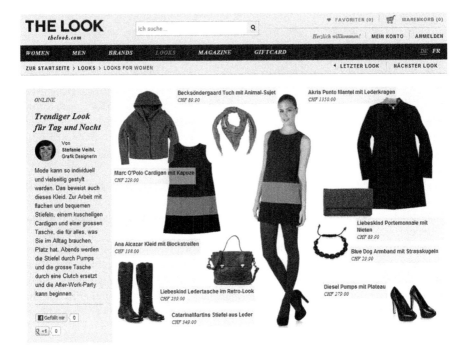

Rich media, such as photo shoots of entire sets and videos, are crucial to communicate the brand value of the Look and the different PKZ brands. The PKZ approach is to sell looks and not just clothes. Therefore a significant investment was made in a separate photo shoot cockpit, as part of the PIM. The photo shoot cockpit allows the organization to plan the entire photography process including planning the shoot, adding models and photographers to a shoot, linking the shots to a product, setting hotspots on the pictures and publishing them online.

For example: the content manager creates "style tips" in the cockpit, adding different SKUs to one style tip. After adding the style tip to a scheduled shoot, the cockpit then calculates which SKUs are shot in which order to reduce unnecessary clothing changes, and in the end production time.

The Cockpits with the respective processes enables PKZ to publish new products within 3 days after arrival. Besides the time to market benefits, PKZ's PIM system also decreases production costs per picture.

When the product is enriched, all information translated and photos added, the product is published automatically.

8.9.5 Looking Back and Forward

Mr. Schibler states: "We are very happy with the way we set up our PIM processes. They allow us to be efficient while still making sure we stay true to our brands. The main lesson learned concerns storage. We underestimated how much hard disc space we would need. We used more terabytes of data in our first year, than we expected to use in 4 years. Another thing we learned is that the back-end graphical user interface had to be adjusted based on the process the people really work with. It's very difficult to define everything upfront. Probably even impossible."

With the Web site up and running, the goal is to extend the number of PIM channels in 2013 with a mobile Web shop. The Look magazine may also use more product data directly from the PIM system.

8.10 Thomas Cook

Product Information Management is a Global Process
  Enri Meijers, Manager Content House

8.10.1 The Organization

Thomas Cook is one of the Largest Travel organizations worldwide with sales of around 12 billion €, 22.3 million customers, 31,000 employees, a fleet of 93 aircraft, and a network of over 3,400 owned and franchised travel stores and interests in 86 hotels and resort properties (Fig. 8.2).

8.10.2 The PIM

In 2008 Thomas Cook West Europe (Belgium, France and the Netherlands), decided to improve its product content management process. Product content is a crucial element in selling holidays, both online as well as via print and in store. The information has to be correct, both to prevent negative surprises for travelers as well as not to undersell a holiday destination. Not only the facts have to be presented, but also the experience a traveler can expect locally. The experience given with the information has to match the actual experience.

In order to do this, Thomas Cook collects a massive amount of data. Not only basic data like hotel name and location, but also its facilities (bar, restaurant) on multiple levels (the hotel itself, its rooms, and hotel surroundings). Photo and video material, maps, customer reviews are all crucial to convey the right customer experience.

Thomas Cook West selected Stibo as product information management system. With the system more than 1,300 destinations (countries, regions, places) and 12,000 accommodations are managed worldwide.

Fig. 8.2 Print catalogs are still an essential channel for Thomas Cook

8.10.3 Sources and Channels

Information is gathered from several sources, e.g. the booking systems of Thomas Cook and external destination content publishers.

The most important source are the accommodation owners themselves. The local Thomas Cook destination management together with the hotel managers make sure all information is updated.

Each entry is validated by the responsible product manager. In addition, the hotel owner is contractually obliged to enter the information correctly and keep it up to date.

The enriched product information is distributed across several channels:
• The different Thomas Cook West Web sites (vrijuit.nl, thomascook.nl, neckermann.nl, thomascook.be, neckermann.be);
• The newsletters of the different brands;
• The print catalogs of the different Thomas Cook brands;
• The internal booking system of the Thomas Cook agencies;
• Resellers of the accommodations e.g. travel agencies and online hotel Web sites.

Complex workflows have been set up to manage this continuously changing database of product information. If a swimming pool is closed for renovation, not only the product managers have to know, but customers may have to be informed.

8.10.4 PIM to Print

Thomas Cook's focus has been on improving the catalog creation process and on publishing information on the Web faster. Every year Thomas Cook West prints many different catalogs, each with an average of 250 pages, 17,500 pages in total. In the past this meant each page had to be designed manually again each year.

Now one designer creates all catalog templates for the three countries using Adobe's Indesign.

Catalogs are no longer designed page by page. Instead the product managers determine which product is shown in which order and to what extent in a very simple format:

1. Hotel A—25 % Page
2. Hotel B—75 % Page
3. Hotel C—200 %

Hotels A and B are placed on one page where Hotel A gets 25 % of the page and B 75 %. Hotel C is so important is gets 2 pages of space. The system then knows which template to use and which data to extract from the PIM system. No manual effort is needed. Competitors still need 10–15 designers to do the same job.

This saves product managers an enormous amount of work. The product manager knows the information in the system is correct as well as the priority in which it is to be placed. The designer can focus on creating templates and not on correcting and retyping errors on pages.

8.10.5 PIM Benefits

Mr. Enri Meijers, manager Content House, has had ultimate responsibility for the PIM process since 2011. Looking back Mr. Meijers cannot conceive of a situation where the PIM process would not have been supported by a system.

More important than the cost reductions achieved, is the fact that Thomas Cook is much better able to manage the quality of its product information. Travelers confronted with hotels not offering the promised facilities quickly demand compensation. The number of complaints has been dramatically reduced with the introduction of the new system.

8.10.6 Organization

Mr. Meijers reports to the CEO of Thomas Cook West. The Content House department focuses on the PIM process. The department has eight developers and functional analysts and four first and second line operational support members. The support team helps the product managers in the different countries to use the PIM system.

The product managers, who determine the assortment of Thomas Cook, are responsible for entering the product data in the system and the quality of the data. Decision about functional changes and new projects are made in a steering committee led by Mr. Meijers. Members are the SPOC (Single Point of Contact) for the PIM process of the different countries.

8.10.7 Lessons Learned

Looking back, Mr. Meijers states that the way the system was set up modeled too much the organizational structure of Thomas Cook West at that time and focused too much on supporting the print process instead of all different sources.

At that time, each country and brand was set up very independently. As a result, a structure was created where each country and brand maintained each accommodation itself. This resulted in each department asking the same accommodation owner to enter their product information into the system, twice or even more often.

Thomas Cook is now changing its structure. Product information maintenance is extended across organizational boundaries to, in the end, collect product information about an accommodation only once within the organization.

Where in the early days the printed catalogs were the only information source for selling and exploring the "holiday emotion", you see nowadays that the brochure is used as one of the information sources. Together with the hotel operator, tour operator, customer reviews and local sites the customers determine their perfect holiday.

The PIM system was set up in a rather crude way for the print catalogs. Product descriptions were entered as text blocks instead of being created based on templates which are filled with attributes. An example:

The description "Hotel Asperia is located directly on the beach. Its facilities include a restaurant, two swimming pools and a bar" can be entered as one text block. The text block has to be translated as a whole and is difficult to maintain (e.g. you have to scan the text if an additional swimming pool is built).

Mr. Meijers says that Thomas Cook is now developing a much more granular set-up of the PIM allowing product data to be separated from the template. An example:

Template: <accommodation_type> <accommodation_name> lies <location>. It offers several facilities amongst which a <number_facility_1> <name_facility_1>, <number_facility_2> <name_facility_2> and <number_facility_3> <name_facility_3>.

The information about the hotel is maintained separately[1]:

- <accommodation_type>: Hotel
- <accommodation_name>: Asperia
- <number_facility_1>: 1
- <name_facility_1>: restaurant
- <number_facility_2>: 2
- <name_facility_2>: swimming pools
- <number_facility_3>: 1
- <name_facility_3>: bar

---

[1] The example is simplified. In practice much more complexity is added. E.g. an "s" has to be added if more than one swimming pool is offered.

The template can be maintained and translated separately as can the facilities. The benefit of creating a much more granular product data model is that it is much more suitable for the Web. For example, customers can search on separate criteria like swimming pool and bar.

Mr. Meijers states: "When we set the PIM up we should have looked more at the future. What is our end goal, and then set up the system with this goal in mind instead of only trying to support the existing way of working. We now know we have to create a lean PIM process, removing duplication of work as much as possible and which is scalable, meaning more products and supported languages does not mean a corresponding growth in manpower to maintain product information. Product information management is a global process".

Appendix II: PIM Software Vendors

9

This chapter briefly examines the PIM solutions of several vendors. It was not possible to go into detail for each supplier neither was it possible contact all vendors, there are simply too many and some did not reply to enquiries.

However, it may be worthwhile investigating several vendors not discussed in this book as they offer special features or focus on specific industries, e.g.[1]:

- AdvancedConcepts
- ASIM
- ComoSoft
- CIC
- Crossbase
- E-pro
- CaTS
- Guide2Media
- Infuniq
- Itestra
- Media Impression
- MyView
- Nexum
- Sepia
- Stampfli
- The PIM company
- Viamedici

9.1   Agility Multichannel Ltd.

Richard Hunt, CEO and Gene Maggard, VP Global Technical Sales

---

[1] Source: among others http://www.pim-verzeichnis.de/

J. Abraham, *Product Information Management*, Management for Professionals,
DOI 10.1007/978-3-319-04885-7_9, © Springer International Publishing Switzerland 2014

9.1.1 The Company

Agility Multichannel's goal is to help companies gather, enrich and deliver consistent product information and branded messages in order to maximize sales.

Agility Multichannel is a relatively new company, founded in 2011 through an MBO from its previous parent, though its PIM product Agility is more than 10 years old. European sales and support are overseen directly from Agility Multichannel's corporate headquarters in York in the United Kingdom, as well as through international partners in France, Switzerland, Germany and Sweden.

Agility Multichannel's fully owned subsidiary, Pindar North America, Inc., was established in 2002 and distributes and supports Agility software in North and South America and Canada.

Key facts	
Founded	MBO in 2011
Employees	50
Customers	75
Main industries	Manufacturing, Distribution, Retail
Turnover (2011)	US$9.1 million
EBIT	US$734,000
Net income	N/A
Solution	Web-based client. SaaS, on premises, or hosted
License structure	From: Monthly SaaS/rental: US$1,500 per month Enterprise: US$50,000 plus 22 % maintenance/enhancements and support

The firm targets companies who manufacture or distribute products, both B2C and B2B. Key technology partners are Adobe, Microsoft, Oracle and IBM. Implementation partners include Axpa (Sweden), IT Gravity GmbH (Germany), Galleio (France), Gartenmann (Switzerland) and ConnectThink (United States).

9.1.2 Proposition

Agility Multichannel's platform, called Agility, allows for any number of categories or hierarchies with an unlimited number of levels. Categories can range from browsing structures for the Web to traditional classification classes. Each product can be categorized in multiple structures as required for different markets, channels, customers, etc.

PIM process	
Master data management	V
Category management	V
Classification and attribute management	V
Unit management	V
Catalog management	V
Data quality management	Ext.

(continued)

Product lifecycle management	X
Publication management	V
Product localization	V
Authorization management	V
PIM 2 Print support	V
Media asset management	V
Workflow management	V
Price management	V
Product enrichment	V
Mass mutations and rollback	V

Category-based attributes allow an administrator to assign product specifications to any level in a category structure, and those attributes can be made to be inherited by certain types of objects that are children of that category or a higher level category. Agility also supports the use of industry standard taxonomies such as UNSPSC, BOSS (office suppliers), etc.

The platform allows for calculated attributes that can perform conversions (such as between decimal and metric values) and can also "mix and match" dimensional attributes. A unit of measure can be held as a separate attribute for data maintenance along with the value but, when required for integration or publishing purposes, a virtual attribute can be used that combines the component parts together and presents it in the desired format. Another type of attribute is "Content Gateway", whereby the attribute value itself is not stored in Agility but is instead retrieved on demand in real time from another system. This type of attribute is especially useful for constantly changing data, such as sales of a product or product inventory levels.

A separate catalog structure enables print catalogs, Web catalogs, email campaigns, etc. Products can be used in any or all of the catalogs and set so that, if information changes, it updates all the places where it resides ("global values"). However, some attributes may also be set to a "local" value, meaning they are valid for only one instance.

Agility offers multiple methods for data quality management. At the basic level, validation rules are offered that can also be extended by custom logic through an API. Multiple choice list options are supported as well as a glossary, to ensure consistency for standard phrases or symbols. Workflow capabilities allow for approvals and changing user access, dependent on the status of a product or category.

Agility supports integration of Pentaho Data Integration ETL and reporting tool, which gives access to data integration, validation and reporting capabilities using the Agility Query Language (AQL). Agility can also connect to other data quality tools and services.

Publication structures, separate from category structures, allow assortments of products to be published to any number of channels. These can be delivered as exports or delivered incrementally as messages via Agility's Syndication Server or queried from a repository of approved product information.

Agility can house product data, pictures and other elements in multiple language versions. Attributes can be set up to be language independent or can have different information, including the values in choice lists. Agility also manages different currencies and the style of displaying currencies (such as the swapping of "," and ".").

Internal tools—such as split screens that show the base language in one screen and the translation in the other—assist in translating languages. For companies that use translation agencies, Agility provides an import/export of the base language in XML to be read into "translation memory" systems such as Trados.

A workflow system is built into Agility. Workflows can be established for products, publications, images and attributes (such as a legal approval for an attribute value). Workflows can be triggered by other workflows. For example: once all products in a category are approved, Agility can automatically move the category workflow to the next step. Workflows are created using a wizard that walks an administrator through the stages of naming the workflow, assigning tasks (or "states"), assigning users or groups of people to each state, and then determining how notifications (email, to-do list) are going to be made when a state is reached.

Agility supports different pricing schemes. At its heart are the concepts of "price lists" which are a set of prices for a given set of products in a given region, and "price types", which allow for many different variants of pricing, such as currency symbols, display preferences, etc., for a particular product within a price list. Through calculated attributes and scripting capabilities called "price styles", Agility can be custom tailored, for example, a percent value off a price as a special offer. As explained previously, Content Gateway enables sales metrics from other systems to be viewed and calculated in Agility.

Mass mutations (or mass updates) are accomplished using either the import and export facilities or ETL and Data Integration tools. For power users, an "Edit in Excel" option is offered.

For print, Agility is integrated with Adobe InDesign and Quark Xpress so that operators can use product templates and other tools to create both print and digital publications. As an alternative to using those platforms, Agility's Visualizer module provides the means to easily create flyers, catalogs and other types of documents without any knowledge of page layout platforms or investment in those clients. Automated PDF generation of the finished result can be used for publications.

9.1.3 Technical Overview

Agility supports both MS SQLServer and Oracle databases and application servers by Oracle (WebLogic) and IBM (WebSphere). Agility is based on Java and Apache on the server side. Java is also the basis for a client side application for super users (admin user, demanding end-users). A separate Web client user interface is offered for normal content management (Fig. 9.1).

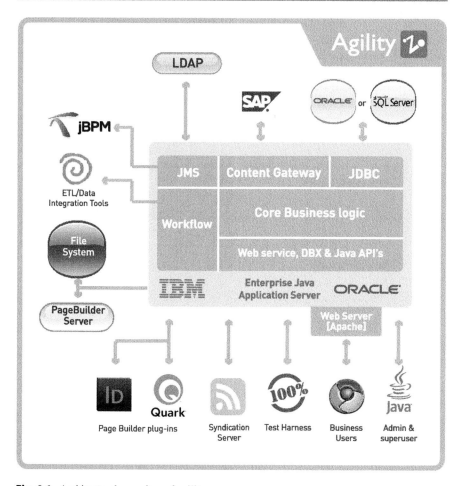

Fig. 9.1 Architectural overview of agility

9.1.4   Why Consider?

Agility Multichannel, with its Agility solution, has a clear vision of what a PIM should do and should not do. Its APIs enable external applications, such as ETL, to be integrated where good solutions already exist. Agility was designed from the outset to easily integrate with other applications, which allows the company to focus on the continuous improvement of the PIM itself.

References	
Distribution	Allied Electronics, Axminster, Office Depot, etc.
Retail	Avon Products, Shop Direct Group, Jula, etc.
Manufacturing	Oriflame, Testo, TTI Group, etc.

With Agility's new Web interface in version 5.2 the company is looking to minimize the complexity of PIM for individual users by allowing them to create their own "workspaces" and "gadgets" for their specific tasks. The company is also bringing down the Total Cost of Ownership (TCO) by streamlining the implementation process (full implementation can take as little as 2 months), offering access to SaaS/rental models, and support of MS SQL Server as an alternative to Oracle. Such solutions and endeavors will prove to be more attractive to smaller as well as some larger companies, and should widen the appeal of PIM to more organizations.

9.2   CONTENTSERV

Koen van den Bossche, General Manager CONTENTSERV Benelux

9.2.1   The Company

Originally founded as a profit center of the German media service provider Kastner AG, in 1999, CONTENTSERV started up as an autonomous software company in 2002 with CEO Patricia Kastner and CTO Alexander Wörl as executives. In 2012 the company turned into an international holding and stock corporation.

Key facts	
Founded	2002
Employees	90
Customers	400
Main industries	Automotive, Production, Finance, Pharmaceuticals, Media
Turnover	Confidential
EBIT	Confidential
Net income	Confidential
Solution	Web-based, SAAS
License structure	Confidential

CONTENTSERV focuses on what it calls Enterprise Marketing Management. Its mission is to simplify marketing processes in product communication by supporting the media-neutral management of content to planning and production across all media up to process control and the ongoing optimization of campaigns.

CONTENTSERV is headquartered in Switzerland and Germany with representatives in Belgium, USA and India. It has created a partner network throughout Europe of about 45 implementation partners and partners overseas in USA, Singapore and Brazil.

The company realized more than 400 customers projects in several industries for companies like Siemens, BMW, LG, Texas Instruments, Miele, VOITH and Bauknecht.

Key Technology Partners are Adobe, Across, SDL Trados, InBetween, WerkII, Talend, First Spirit and Magento.

9.2.2 Proposition

CONTENTSERV provides not only a PIM solution, but offers a much broader solution for marketing production and management. The processes the company tries to cover are:

- Integrating and enriching the marketing content (products, media assets, editorial content and customers/target groups);
- Planning, production, correction, adaptation and distribution of page-based output (catalogs, campaigns, sales documentation, datasheets,...);
- Managing and monitoring budgets, campaigns, teams and resources;

PIM process	
Master data management	V
Category management	V
Classification and attribute management	V
Unit management	V
Catalog management	V
Data quality management	V
Product lifecycle management	P
Publication management	V
Product localization	V
Authorization management	V
PIM 2 Print support	V
Media asset management	V
Workflow management	V
Price management	V
Product enrichment	V
Mass mutations and rollback	V

CONTENTSERV integrates into several systems to complete its offering:

- with MDM and CMS systems for providing master data to build on;
- with Web-CMS and E-Shop systems for data-driven, automated communication channels;
- with sales automation and CRM systems to distribute, monitor and improve campaigns.

The PIM module of CONTENTSERV supports all the basic PIM processes. PIM objects are organized in recursive "category" folders as master data structure, which is also used for inheritance of product features. On top of this, product search lists can be organized in "Views". Views can be organized by drag and drop and set up alternative category structures for Web deployment, publication structures, etc.

Attributes are m-to-n assigned to classes. Classes again can be organized in class-trees and inherit these assignments. Products finally have one (possibly inherited) class and then show all class attributes.

Unit measurement is supported as well via a measurement unit attribute type and an administration of units. Display of measures and units is based on the user interface language, where values are recalculated accordingly (like pounds to kg).

Catalog structures are built up either through views and then exported as XML, CSV or sent through integrated rendering engines like InBetween. Another approach is to assign products to catalogs in the creative approach, where products are placed in documents, while CONTENTSERV keeps track of the usage and relations.

Prices are covered by a special price data type. Alternatively, a sub-table-like attribute is available that can be configured to hold pricelists with customized features, like valid-from and until, etc.

Data quality management is supported via extended search results that can be stored in Favorites for review. Workflows and data restrictions make sure that data is entered in the required form, sequence and quality and that translation processes are completed.

CONTENTSERV comes with a large set of features and modules around Publication Management. The PPM (Print Production Manager) module makes it possible to organize multiple InDesign or PDF documents and combine them into one publication. The PPM InDesign Editor allows Web-based editing of InDesign Files. The PPM Comet Connector allows Graphics Designers at InDesign Clients to connect to CS, and Comet Connector allows Graphics Designers at InDesign Clients to connect to CS and download or upload InDesign Files. PIM data can be made available in the InDesign Client and can be placed using templates. CS comes with its own CS Media Asset Management System. MAM assets can be searched and embedded into InDesign files.

The CONTENTSERV Translation Manager module allows users to translate products workflow based by bundling them into translation jobs. Translation Jobs can be pre-translated using the translation memory of previous jobs, translated in the user interface or sent to external TMS (Translation Management System) like Trados or Across (Fig. 9.2).

9.2.3 Technical Overview

CONTENTSERV works with several operating systems e.g. Linux (e.g. Red Hat Enterprise, Debian, Ubuntu), Microsoft Windows Server 2008 R2 and Apple Max OS X Server 10.5 and higher. The application itself runs on PHP and MySQL. CONTENTSERV is a Web-based application allowing it to run from most browsers (recommended: Firefox 3–9 and 11–16, MS Internet Explorer 8 and 9 (with current release CS13), Google Chrome 11 and Apple Safari 5) (Fig. 9.3).

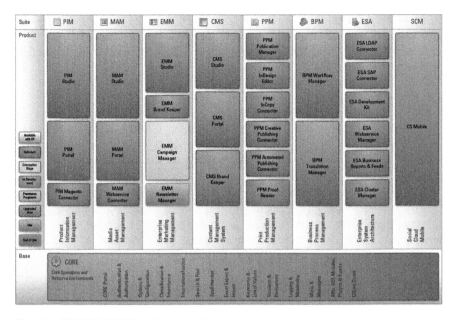

Fig. 9.2 CONTENTSERV product overview

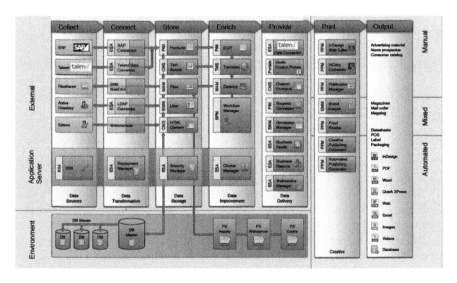

Fig. 9.3 CONTENTSERV CS13.0 architecture

9.2.4   Why Consider?

CONTENTSERV strives for a market position as "one-stop-shop" for all publishing needs in marketing.

Key references	
Automotive	BMW, Lemken
Production	Bosch, Siemens, LG Electronics, Texas Instruments,
Media	Weltbild, Lukkien, Worldguide, etc.
Other	BMW, DZ Bank, Roche, etc.

Where some hardcore MDM/PIM software vendors have invested heavily in data import/export and ETL features, CONTENTSERV focuses on integrating with third party tools like Talend, jCatalog, e-pro and Myview. Likewise, classification models like ETIM and eCl@ss are not supported out-of-the-box and data quality audits and supplier on-boarding features are limited.

CONTENTSERV may therefore not be the logical choice for wholesalers and retailers working with hundreds of thousands of products whose data is mainly provided by suppliers. For brand owners, production and marketing companies with a more limited product set but complex and international product marketing communication processes, CONTENTSERV is a solution to be investigated.

9.3   Eggheads

Michael Henrichs, Director of Sales and member of the board

9.3.1   The Company

Eggheads is a German PIM system software provider founded in 1990. Their mission is to provide a professional multichannel product communication platform based on standard software.

The company operates in six countries (Germany, Austria, Switzerland, France, Netherlands, Belgium), has 35 employees, 50 customers and around 5,000 active users.

Eggheads does not have a specific target industry as they propose PIM solutions tailored for small customers (2 users/1,000 products), up to large multinational organizations (more than 200 users, five million products, one million media assets, in 30+ languages). The company is privately owned.

Key facts	
Founded	1990
Employees	35
Customers	5,000

(continued)

Main industries	Travel, Fashion
Turnover (2010/11)	No data provided
EBIT	No data provided
Net income	No data provided
Solution	Fat and Web-based client. Saas, on site, hosted offering
License structure	Based on modules, no. of interfaces, concurrent users and languages

9.3.2   Proposition

Eggheads cmi24 platform is the basis for product communication and cross media publishing. The platform consists of over 50 different modules.

The core of the cmi24 platform is its PIM module. The PIM module supports the management of master data in multiple languages, the creation of classification classes and categories. Optional modules are export configuration and versioning.

PIM process	
Master data management	V
Category management	V
Classification and attribute management	V
Unit management	X
Catalog management	V
Data quality management	V
Product lifecycle management	V
Publication management	V
Product localization	V
Authorization management	V
PIM 2 Print support	V
Media asset management	Ext.
Workflow management	V
Price management	V
Product enrichment	V
Mass mutations and rollback	V

The workflow management module features the creation of tasks, assigning them to a user and informing the user by email.

A special module has been created to allow external users to add or update product information. New information can first be approved before it is actually added to the PIM.

The shop module offers an out-of-the-box e-commerce Web site. The module allows adaption of the graphical user interface and supports several payment methods.

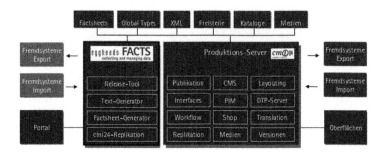

Fig. 9.4 Functional overview of Eggheads platform

A special module is the FACTS module which allows users to enter data offline and synchronize with the central database. External classification classes like BMEcat and Etim are supported.

The MAM module is internal. The module offers features like photo tagging and rendering the photo resolution and size to the right channel formats.

The platform offers an import module with drag and drop functionality for field mapping. Standard export interfaces supported include the TYPO3 CMS and desk top publishing (DTP) software like QuarkXPress and Adobe InDesign.

The print module is used among others by TUI and Thomas Cook to create over 50,000 pages of travel catalogs each year. It has a WYSIWYG-editor to directly edit pre-PDF pages.

For mobile, Egghead has developed two standard applications (for IOS and Android) which allows customers to quickly create their own app with a product catalog.

9.3.3   Technical Overview

The Egghead platform is based on Java, Eclipse framework and SQL-DB (Fig. 9.4).

9.3.4   Why Consider?

Egghead distinguishes itself by providing a complete solution including important features like Media Asset Management and PIM2Print for a relatively low price. It has built an impressive reference base, particularly in the travel industry.

References	
Travel	TUI, Thomas Cook, Hafermann Reisen, vTours and FTI Touristik
Fashion	Mammut, Schuster, Mewa
Other	Channel21, Koziol, Naber, Sutterlüty, Schüller

9.4   Enterworks

Warren Jones, VP Marketing

Key facts	
Founded	1996
Employees	60
Customers	200
Main industries	Distribution/wholesale
Turnover	Not public
EBIT	Not public
Net income	Not public
Solution	Web-based, hosted, cloud and on-premises
License structure	Both enterprise-level and flexible subscription models are offered

9.4.1   The Company

Enterworks started in 1996 with data integration for global intelligence agencies. As a result the company has gained significant experience in handling complex data integrations. Enterworks moved into the PIM arena after integrating its content management and enterprise workflow solutions.

Enterworks offers "Enterworks Enable", an enterprise platform for managing content and digital assets and publishing them to multiple channels and media. Enable creates a central repository of data from multiple sources, where the data can be managed, enriched, and dynamically syndicated to multiple users and applications.

Enterworks serves the US and Canadian market directly by own-owned offices. Europe is served through representatives. All implementations, however, are done only with Enterworks' employees. Enterworks is privately owned.

9.4.2   Proposition

Enterworks Enable supports all the standard PIM processes like master data, category, classification and unit management. For unstructured content, Enable has its own Digital Asset Management (DAM) module.

In general the Enterworks system is very fine grained. For example, Enable is very flexible in the creation and management of an unlimited number of attributes, which can be associated with multiple related objects, such as product, item, brand, vendor, and more. In addition, within the product a concept for "time effectivity" of a product is offered. For example, a user can establish that a new product is to be introduced on a given date, in a given set of available colors. On a subsequent date, several colors will be discontinued and several added, and on yet another date the product as a whole will be retired.

PIM process	
Master data management	V
Category management	V
Classification and attribute management	V
Unit management	V
Catalog management	V
Data quality management	V
Product lifecycle management	V
Publication management	V
Product localization	V
Authorization management	P
PIM 2 Print support	V
Media asset management	V
Workflow management	P
Price management	V
Product enrichment	V
Mass mutations and rollback	V

A point where Enterworks feels it excels is importing product data from thousands of suppliers, managing and converting data, and distributing it in target-specific formats.

The Enable Portal Framework lets the user create and manage portals that allow distributors, dealers, suppliers, and customers to access product information, manage their accounts, and other tasks. Enable's easy-to-configure capabilities let customers select the features they want, set the roles that allow certain participants to create, publish, and access product data and digital assets, administer the business rules governing pricing and promotions, and perform other functions for creating a productive and secure working environment for partners and customers.

The platform supports importing and mapping of inbound content, down to the individual attribute level, from files, databases, and other systems. Enable supports direct database access and operational system integration, using file-based and Web service-based means. All system objects can be imported (or exported) as spreadsheet entities, including the creation of a full system migration file. In addition, Enable provides multiple levels of configuration for the scheduling and execution of bulk import processes.

The data quality system includes business-level rules (price increases limited to x percent per month) and data-level rules (data typing and data assignment) that greatly reduce or eliminate errors in product content. This allows the automatic validation of data provided by suppliers, e.g. a flag can be raised when a product price is imported with a value 40 % below its earlier value as this may indicate a data entry error.

An essential part of mass data import is the workflow functionality Enterworks offers. For many Enterworks customers, a key process used for correcting data errors is the Enable workflow, which automatically routes items to the appropriate person for approval and highlights processing exceptions that need immediate

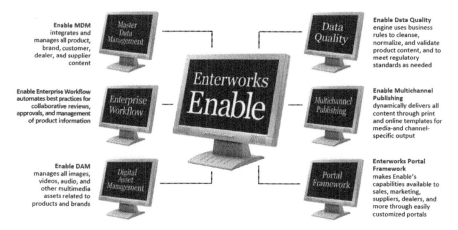

Fig. 9.5 Functional overview Enterworks

attention. The rules can be executed en masse on an entire set of data, or automatically applied every time a product record is opened and saved (Fig. 9.5).

Enterworks is very proud of its workflow engine. Enable doesn't rely on hardcoded workflows that require customers to adapt their business processes; a drag-and-drop interface even lets users model business processes themselves. A graphical status monitoring tool displays the number of activities at each flow, and the location of bottlenecks so that optimization steps can be taken quickly.

Enable also offers PIM 2 Print support. The software dynamically links the repository-based content to print page templates and artwork. Users can manage an unlimited number of style and document templates, update product data within documents, and perform other print publishing tasks. Enable's Adobe InDesign Plug-In supports document layout with real-time integration of content from the central repository, and write-back privileges for authorized users. Automatic pagination and indexing allows the user, with a click of a button, to flow content into documents and automatically build an index. Drag-and-drop technology allows products to be allocated to page layouts, and the page or spread to be rendered in real time.

Product enhancements planned for 2013 include new capabilities in the user interface and navigation, DAM and MDM integration, planning and product management, and marketing asset management.

9.4.3 Technical Overview

Enterworks does not use third party solutions. The Enable solution is coded in Java, JavaScript, and C#. SQL Server is typically used for database storage for the PIM and workflow capabilities.

From a physical standpoint, three tiers (Web, application, data) can be distributed across a customer's enterprise. Several caching techniques (Ajax, jQuery) are employed to ensure that the interaction at browser level is acceptable. Much of the data is stored as XML in order to maintain flexibility for customers as they both initially define their model and maintain it on an ongoing basis.

Two features are provided to further enhance data retrieval when necessary—"snapshot" attributes and "Empower" tables. Snapshot attributes are attributes that live in the XML structure but are extracted as they are saved, placed in a snapshot table, and indexed for high-speed search and retrieval. With Empower, a complete set of relational tables is automatically maintained that represent a direct reflection of the XML structure for high transaction scenarios.

9.4.4   Why Consider

Enterworks has a clear and strong focus on distributors and wholesalers in business products, electronics, medical suppliers and more. As a result is has invested significantly in data import, portal, data quality features from product manufacturers which makes it an interesting choice for comparable companies.

References	
Distribution	United Stationers, NRHA, HDW, E&R Industrial, Owens & Minor, Johnstone Supply, Orgill
Other	Synthes, Darden Restaurants

9.5   Heiler Software AG

Benjamin Rund, Chief Marketing Officer

9.5.1   The Company

Heiler Software AG was founded in 1987 by Rolf Heiler who is still the company CEO. The company is listed on the Frankfurt Stock Exchange in the General Standard Segment. The company headquarters is in Stuttgart (Germany). It has sales offices in Detroit (USA), Toronto (Canada) and Sydney (Australia).

Key facts	
Founded	1987
Employees	150
Customers	170 (PIM)
Main industries	Retail, wholesale, Manufacturing
Turnover (2011/12)	19,685,000 €

(continued)

EBIT	101
Net income	450
Solution	Rich Client/Server on site/on premises/100 % Web data and process access
License structure	250 k €–850 k € details on request

Heiler focuses on the retail, wholesale (distribution) and manufacturing industries and within these particularly on consumer electronics, fashion, food, industrial supply/MRO, healthcare and media.

End 2012 US-based Informatica Corporation announced its decision to launch through its subsidiary Informatica Deutschland AG a voluntary public takeover offer to acquire all outstanding shares in Heiler Software AG. As of March 2013 Informatica holds about 98 % of shares.

9.5.2   Proposition

Heiler's vision is to connect people and data, easily. With an immense increase in data volumes, and more complexity and speed, the crucial thing in the future will be to connect information and data with the right people, tailored to their roles and needs. It is a question of data and people, not of systems.

Data and information will become the most critical differentiator in any competition. Turning data into business means not only delivering standard software, but it also means more solutions to solve and improve better business processes.

PIM process	
Master data management	V
Category management	V
Classification and attribute management	V
Unit management	X
Catalog management	V
Data quality management	V
Product lifecycle management	V
Publication management	V
Product localization	V
Authorization management	V
PIM 2 Print support	V
Media asset management	V
Workflow management	V
Price management	V
Product enrichment	V
Mass mutations and rollback	V

Heiler Enterprise PIM provides companies with a central repository for all product data for the purpose of distribution in all sales channels (e-commerce, mobile, social, print, and more).

One of the features that make Heiler special is its choice for a Windows-based interface as rich client for complex data management tasks. It offers features many product entry specialists are addicted to, such as dragging and dropping products into categories, copying "cells", etc. Likewise, multiple views are supported e.g. table and form views. Where other systems sometimes have difficulty supporting mass edit features, this is no problem for Heiler due to its choice of interface.

With PIM 7 all processes from supplier onboarding, data search, editing, data quality management and digital asset management, are available as Web access.

The system supports multiple product hierarchies, each with its own user roles access rights. Apart from creating multiple classification systems yourself several standard classification systems are supported, including eCl@ss, ETIM, UNSPSC, ProfiCl@ss, etc.

Price management supports regional pricing, tiered pricing, modeling of price validity periods, different currencies, surcharges and discount groups.

Heiler offers several features to reduce the work effort, such as preset values defined on structure group level when maintaining product/item attributes, automatic recalculation of attribute values (e.g. size, units etc.) during import and export with respect to a specified structure system, etc.

With its supplier portal and extensive processes and functions for data integration, Heiler Product Information Management (PIM) ticks all the boxes for ensuring optimized data quality in large assortments. A central cockpit is offered to manage imports from different sources. Structured file format (text, Excel, CSV, XML, BMECat, iDoc, etc.) can be mapped to the master data model using a visual editor (drag and drop). Validations and transformations can be configured in the import.

Heiler has invested considerable effort on data quality management via profiling (analyzing the quality of incoming data), firewalling (prevent poor quality data from entering the PIM system), cleansing and enrichment (identify inconsistencies in the data), matching and merging incoming product data with already existing records. This allows data from multiple suppliers of the same product to be merged into a "best of breed" record. An audit trail module is available for tracking the change history of every object. Heiler Enterprise PIM—Data Quality delivers an integrated solution, designed for managing data quality of product and supplier data, including the support for data integration, data profiling and data governance. It enables companies to implement consistent, re-usable and automated data quality processes for product data, throughout the entire data lifecycle. Informatica's Data Quality Solution is an integral part of PIM 7 and has been positioned in Magic Quadrant for Data Quality Tools, report by Gartner, Ted Friedman, August 8, 2012.

Heiler has a built-in export template editor that makes it possible to configure the output format without programming. The same flexibility as in the import cockpit is available in the export template editor. Through the UI, the export formats can be configured including validity checks and data transformations. Channel validations and transformations can be set up in the UI so that any output format can be produced in a well-formed and efficient way (e.g. HTML, Excel, XML, CSV, Text, etc.).

The system has an integrated Media Asset Management system. Digital assets (images, videos, PDF, etc.) can be imported and automatically or manually associated with products. Products can have multiple assets associated, qualified by the locale, asset type (e.g. front or rear view) and asset quality (e.g. high-res image, thumbnail, etc.). Workflows for creating derivatives and versions of media assets can be created.

9.5.3 Technical Overview

Heiler's PIM system is based on a three tier architecture (DB, Application Server, Client) with additional modules running on separate servers (e.g. DAM, Audit Trail, Web applications). Its software is built using standard technologies e.g. Java/Java EE, Spring, OSGi (Equinox), Eclipse RCP, Hibernate, Apache Solr, Apache Axis2, Activiti, GWT, Apache Tomcat, Quartz. As DB platforms Oracle and Microsoft SQL Server are supported.

9.5.4 Why Consider?

Heiler has a clear focus on Product Information Management. As a result it is one of the more extensive systems on the market with its own MAM, supplier portal and data quality solution as integral part.

References	
Retail	Otto, Direct Group, Hornbach, Edeka, Lidl, Saks Fifth Avenue
Wholesale	Lawson, Eriks, Fastenal, Kramp, Otello, Pietsch
Production	Abus, Puma, Roche, Werner, Rubbermaid, Tommy Hilfiger
Other	

Heiler also offers a B2B e-commerce system, however this is less advanced than systems like hybris, IBM and Oracle ATG. The company therefore as offers preconfigured integrations for e-commerce solutions like Intershop, IBM, Oracle ATG, Demandware.

Likewise, if offers plug-ins to print solutions like LIS Suite/RS MediaGroup AG, priint:comet/Werk II and Xactuell/codeware. Heiler plans to keep on investing in product information management with special focus on collaboration, integrations and master data management.

9.6   hybris Software (SAP)

9.6.1   The Company

hybris is headquartered in Munich, Germany and delivers OmniCommerce™: enterprise software and on-demand solutions for master data management and commerce processes that give a business a single view of its customers, products and orders, and its customers a single view of the business. hybris helps retailers, manufacturers, distributors, telcos and publishers of software, games and digital media to innovate, sell more and create perpetual digital relationships with their customers. hybris was founded in 1997 by Carsten Thoma, Moritz Zimmermann and Klaas Hermanns and is a privately held company.

Key facts	
Founded	1997
Employees	655+
Customers	450+
Main industries	Retail, wholesale, Manufacturing, Services and Telecommunication
Turnover	Not public
EBIT	Not public
Net income	Not public
Solution	Web-based, on site or SAAS
License structure	Starting at 60,000 €. Depended on no. of cores, users and additional modules (e.g. print, workflow, DAM)

The name hybris derives from Greek literature and describes actions of those who challenged the gods or their laws with ambition and pride.

On August 22, 2011 it was announced that hybris had acquired Canadian company iCongo. The acquisition allowed hybris to expand more rapidly on the American market and expand its suite with, amongst other things, order and warehouse management functionality.

Both Gartner and Forrester rank hybris as a "leader" and list its commerce platform among the top two or three in the market. Over 400 companies have chosen hybris, including many well-known global brands (B2C and B2B).

hybris has sales offices in Germany, Austria, Switzerland, the United Kingdom, France, Italy, Spain, Sweden, the Netherlands, USA, Canada, Brazil, China, Japan and Australia.

As this book was going to press, hybris was acquired by SAP.

PIM process	
Master data management	V
Category management	V
Classification and attribute management	V
Unit management	V
Catalog management	V

(continued)

Data quality management	V
Product lifecycle management	V
Publication management	V
Product localization	V
Authorization management	V
PIM 2 Print support	V
Media asset management	Ext.
Workflow management	V
Price management	V
Product enrichment	V
Mass mutations and rollback	V

9.6.2   Proposition

As the hybris vision is to enable organizations to sell and communicate consistently across all channels and touch points, its Product Content Management (PCM) solution has a central place in hybris' proposition and architecture. In fact, hybris originally started as a PIM software vendor and expanded into the e-commerce/multichannel ecosphere around 2004.

Since then hybris has expanded its offering to several other software solutions like B2C and B2B Commerce, Print, Mobile, Customer Service, Order Management, WCMS, etc.

As PIM functionality has for a long time been the core of what hybris offers, it can be considered more than an extensive software module. The application is also sold stand alone. All major PIM processes are supported.

hybris supports the creation of multiple catalogs, categories and classification trees.

As an international system engineered in Europe, hybris was set up from the start to support product localization, management of prices, taxes and promotions across multiple countries, languages and currencies. It offers workflows to support the translation and product enrichment process. Likewise, external classification systems like ETIM, eClass, UN/SPSC and proficlass are supported.

For organizations with high volumes of products and content-heavy files, hybris offers multi-threaded import capabilities, which speed up the import process.

As hybris' focus is multichannel commerce it also supports typical e-commerce needs like creating relations between products for up- and cross-selling and product reviews.

It has strongly integrated an external DAM system called Celum to support the management of images, graphics and videos. Assets can easily be converted into the desired output format and linked to specific products.

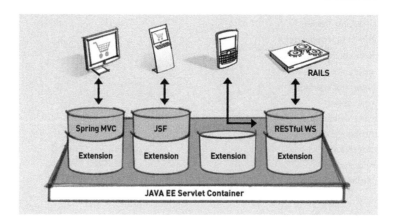

Fig. 9.6 hybris Architecture overview

In the last 2 years hybris has focused on improving the usability of its software with a separate cockpit for importing product data and for maintaining product data. This allows the administrator to work in the hybris Management Console (hMC), an environment that allows all complex transactions while product data entry employees can focus on their work and are not hampered by additional complexity. As the front-end of the hybris suite is Web based, making its solution highly suitable for an international, distributed organization, hybris offers: Perpetual (core based), Subscription (2–5 years) and OnDemand. Licenses can be run on-premises (data center), hosted by hybris (managed service) and OnDemand (license&hosting).

9.6.3   Technical Overview

The execution environment for the hybris platform is a Java EE Servlet Container. Because hybris doesn't require a Java EE server like JBoss, WebLogic, or Websphere, users benefit from lower costs and less complexity. Running on a wide range of operating systems, such as Microsoft Windows, Apple Mac OS X Server, or various other Unix-based operating systems, the hybris platform ships with a preconfigured, production ready Tomcat & tcServer. Alternatively it can be configured for Oracle WebLogic or IBM WebSphere. hybris uses open source technologies such as Spring, ZK, SOLR/Lucene, ANT, Groovy, Apache Commons and many more and regularly releases updates and keeps the technologies current, so you can always enjoy working with the most up-to-date version.

The persistence layer provides fast and reliable CRUD operations and can support, according to hybris, millions of products, customers, prices or any other items in real-time (systems in production support over 100 million price rows). The platform scales linearly to support even those systems with very high traffic (systems in production support over 6,000 inquiries per second) (Fig. 9.6).

9.6.4 Why Consider?

The hybris PIM solution differentiates itself from that of competitors by being completely integrated in an e-commerce platform. In the last few years hybris focused on expanding its suite with related functionality either by acquisition (Order Management of iCongo) or alliances (Digital Asset Management with Celum). hybris accelerated this functional growth in 2012 with, among other things, cooperation with Adobe for content management.

hybris' use of entity data models enables easier management of packaging variations, as well as rapid and flexible bundling of products, or even disaggregation. This is especially useful with digital products and services, where content can be aggregated into a book or journal or disaggregated into chapters, articles, or even images within an article. hybris PCM is built to scale. It is in production on some of the largest B2B and B2C sites hosting millions of products and handling millions of customers.

While the hybris' PIM solution can be acquired stand alone, most companies chose hybris because of the complete omnichannel solution it offers.

Customer references are not published but are available on request at sales@hybris.com.

9.7 IBM

9.7.1 The Company

IBM is a global technology company headquartered in Armonk, NY. It is the largest technology and consulting employer in the world, with approximately 427,000 employees serving clients in 170 countries.

Key facts	
Founded	1911
Employees	433,362
Customers	No information provided
Main industries	No information provided
Turnover 2011	$106.9 billion
Net income 2011	$15.9 billion
Solution	Client/Server, Hosted inhouse
License structure	No information provided

IBM offers a wide range of technology and consulting services; a broad portfolio of middleware for collaboration, predictive analytics, software development and systems management; and advanced servers and supercomputers.

Its PIM-related solution is called IBM InfoSphere Master Data Management Collaboration Server, also known as MDMCS.

9.7.2   Proposition

IBM's PIM solution is strongly based on MDM. Core information of the products required is typically imported from product sources like suppliers or ERP systems.

MDMCS has been developed to support the entire Product Information Management cycle through sourcing, marketing, selling, service and decommissioning of products and services. Embedded workflow ensures true collaboration across divisions. Integration with most Standard ERP applications and import/export functions is supported. Multiple category trees can be set up to support Web navigation, publication structuring, classification, reporting, prices, etc.

PIM process	
Master data management	V
Category management	V
Classification and attribute management	V
Unit management	X
Catalog management	V
Data quality management	V
Product lifecycle management	V
Publication management	V
Product localization	X
Authorization management	V
PIM 2 Print support	Ext.
Media asset management	Ext.
Workflow management	V
Price management	V
Product enrichment	V
Mass mutations and rollback	V

Inheritance of selected attributes is supported for a product, depending on the hierarchy it belongs to. MDMCS has no limitation on unit management or depth of units in packaging. Articles, products, services can be grouped in as many catalogs as required by the business. A catalog can be considered as a business view on articles.

To manage data quality, in addition to internal control mechanisms, MDMCS can be complemented by InfoSphere Information Server for Data Quality. This provides users and data stewards with a suite of data quality management tooling ranging from business glossary to information analysis tools. The suite contains a common Metadata repository and ETL parts to ensure integration.

MDMCS is capable of distinguishing between "going out of assortment" and "end-of-service" date definitions.

Publications can be structured as assortments of products which can be published in several formats (PDF, HTML, XLS, DOC, XML, CSV, ...) and sent to customers over output channels or other systems.

The offering does not include a MAM solution but URLs can be stored to pinpoint to an external location. Workflow is an integral part of the solution. For advanced workflow process management, integration support with existing workflow tools is supported, or IBM Workflow solutions such as ILOG or Lombardi are used.

Price calculations can be made in MDMCS. However, IBM recommends keeping pricing at that central location and replicates recommended retail price as an attribute to the PIM system.

Mass updates (column style) can be performed in MDMCS and do not require export to external personal tools such as Excel.

For PIM2Print IBM claims to offer preprint integration with several packages on the market. Likewise, IBM states it supports most industry standards for classification.

By deploying Information Server as complement to MDMCS, standard interfacing to several ERP and CRM systems are supported.

9.7.3 Technical Overview

MDMCS version 10.0.runs on AIX, Linux (Red Hat or SUSE, Solaris and Windows. Supported databases are DB2, Oracle 11. Underlying Webservers can be Apache. The client side is Microsoft based. Websphere Message Queu is required as messaging software.

MDMCS has a component-based architecture that can consist of a two-tier or three-tier configuration. These components include: core components, integration components, and collaboration components as shown in the figure below.

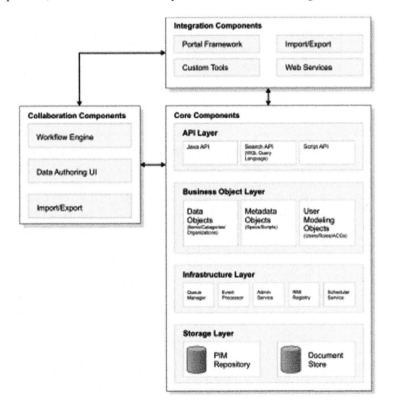

9.7.4 Why Consider?

MDMCS is a solution that borders on the MDM area as the name itself indicates. It is not clear to what extent localization, MDM and product enrichment processes are supported compared with other solutions described in this book.

9.8 INCONY

9.8.1 The Company

INCONY considers itself to be one of the pioneers of PIM. Management started to work in the field of product information management and cross media publishing in 1996, as a department of Siemens Nixdorf. In 2000, the management team founded their own company by a management buy-out.

Key facts	
Founded	2000
Employees	50
Customers	100
Main industries	Technical sectors such as automotive, electronics, mechanics
Turnover	Not public
EBIT	Not public
Net income	Not public
Solution	Web-based; installed on site or hosted
License structure	The user pays per module so that investments can be made step-by-step. Project costs are often below 100,000 € and may start at 20,000 €

INCONY's mission is to enhance and optimize the processes in companies related to product data, to images and the processes to create print documents (catalogs, price lists, data sheets,...), electronic catalogs, Web shops, mobile apps, and several different external formats (Excel, CSV, XML, etc.).

INCONY has centralized its development and sales resources in Germany but supports some 100 customers worldwide (Europe, but also USA, Mexico, China, etc.).

INCONY has customers of different sizes and branches. Most customers are from technical sectors such as automotive, electronics, mechanics, agriculture. Others work in the fashion, lifestyle or publishing industries.

Key partners of INCONY are IBM, Mediaprint, Lightwerk, DVSE, Antenna-House and RenderX.

9.8.2 Proposition

INCONY's PIM system is called ANTEROS. Product data and images can be maintained quite efficiently in ANTEROS and data can also be imported from other systems. Data should only be updated once and not on multiple islands, which enhances the data quality. From the centrally maintained product data and images, print documents can be generated fully automatically, but ANTEROS also provides modules for a Web catalog, a Web shop or app but also to export the data in different formats.

ANTEROS consists of several modules:

- ANTEROS.pim: the central maintenance of product data;
- ANTEROS.im: the administration of images, image search and conversion;
- ANTEROS.ip: an image portal where registered users can search and download images in different formats;
- ANTEROS.imex: to connect third-party systems via XML, CSV or Excel to ANTEROS and to import/export data in almost any combination for other purposes;
- ANTEROS.ws: to deeply integrate a third party system to ANTEROS by Web-services.
- ANTEROS.tsl: for translation support;
- ANTEROS.wf: for workflow-based business processes;
- ANTEROS.print: to generate print catalogs, price lists etc. with chosen data and images;
- ANTEROS.web: creates Web catalogs, Web shops and apps
- ANTEROS.cd: creates CD catalogs;
- ANTEROS.spare: offers functions for spare part catalogs such as hot spots in drawings or definitions in parts lists;

PIM process	
Master data management	V
Category management	V
Classification and attribute management	V
Unit management	V
Catalog management	V
Data quality management	V
Product lifecycle management	P
Publication management	V
Product localization	V
Authorization management	V
PIM 2 Print support	V
Media asset management	V
Workflow management	V
Price management	P
Product enrichment	V
Mass mutations and rollback	V

ANTEROS supports in essence all key PIM processes like Master Data Management, Categorization, Classification, Unit Management, Product enrichment, etc. Also more advanced features like Mass Mutation are supported via a Web interface. All major external classification systems (ETIM, eCl@ss) are supported in all major versions (e.g. eCl@ss 5.0, 6.1,...). In addition ANTEROS provides a media database with Web-based access to images, videos, documents, etc.

INCONY considers itself to be technology leader in print-on-demand. Complex catalogs (see catalog pages below) can be generated completely automatically without the need to finish the catalog in DTP products like Adobe InDesign or Quarck Express. INCONY customers reported that they saved up to 90 % of time and costs in their catalog creation.

The assortment for a publication can be defined on different data levels (product, product family, categories, in short, on any tree level). Print publications can also be defined on demand by a query or collection, e.g. to define an excerpt of a catalog for an offer or to define a customer-specific catalog. Publications in structured files (e.g. in CSV/Excel) can be defined by predefined or self-defined export profiles and arbitrarily combined data (realized by flexible rules) can be exported.

ANTEROS provides its own translation support but also works together with systems such as Trados and Across. ANTEROS' own translation support allows translation of only those texts that have been changed since the previous translation. It provides functions in Web forms and by Excel. The Excel option exports all texts that are required for translation in at least three columns, for example: one for the old English text, one for the new English text, and a third for the translation text that corresponds to the old English text, e.g. German. Colors highlight what has been modified so that that the changes are also visible in Excel.

9.8.3   Technical Overview

The back-end system is Java based and the frontend is dynamically generated in HTML using JSP/JSF (so that no installation or reloading on client computers is required). The database is configured through a JDBC interface and several relational databases can be used (e.g. Oracle, MS SQL, DB2, MySQL). Interfaces towards several ERP systems (SAP, Navision, ProAlpha) are supported via standard APIs.

9.8.4   Why Consider

INCONY supports all core PIM processes. However, its solution distinguishes itself by offering its own Print and DAM solution. While other PIM vendors often depend on integration software and external DTP solutions like Adobe Indesign and Quarck Express, INCONY provides an integrated solution. As a result, INCONY has a very strong track record in print.

References	
Automotive	Hella, Honeywell, Luk, Textar, Stahlgruber
Electronics	Obeta, Fischer Elektronik, Jean Müller, Schwaiger
Tools	Mitutoyo, Beck, Thieme
Others	Heraeus, Simona, Raytheon, Bogner

9.9 ITB

Yvonne Waldbröl, Project Manager

Key facts	
Founded	1996
Employees	45
Customers	82
Main industries	Medium-sized production and wholesale companies
Turnover	Not public
EBIT	Not public
Net income	Not public
Solution	Client Server or ASP, Shop and ConnectPro Web-based
License structure	Starting at 50,000 €

9.9.1 The Company

ITB's mission is to provide an easy way for its customer's customer to buy. The company's headquarters is based in Germany with a project office for customers in Switzerland.

ITB targets medium-sized companies (100 employees and more) which sell or produce a wide variety of standard articles e.g. screws, clothing, cylinders, fittings, tubes.

The company offers three product ranges:
- MeDaPro: a PIM offering;
- TradePro: an Internet Shop with Procurement features, a scanning solution, content management, OCI Interface, Payment option and mobile option;
- ConnectPro: an interface tool offering mapping features and supporting several EDI formats and other import/export formats.

Key partners of ITB are FactFinder (search) and several ERP software vendors. The company is privately owned.

9.9.2 Proposition

ITB offers a PIM system that covers most PIM processes. The user can create its own database fields for article attributes and group them according to product categories in classes. These fields can be handed down (inherited) to other articles.

PIM process	
Master data management	V
Category management	V
Classification and attribute management	V
Unit management	P
Catalog management	V
Data quality management	P
Product lifecycle management	P
Publication management	V
Product localization	V
Authorization management	V
PIM 2 Print support	V
Media asset management	P
Workflow management	V
Price management	P
Product enrichment	V
Mass mutations and rollback	P

The user can also build a product tree according to specific needs. This tree can be copied or adapted for every target client. Products are also grouped and can be provided with individual or handing-down fields. Every knot may contain additional category information.

A product assortment can be created by the user and linked to layout templates that are created in MeDaPro Publish (InDesign based). The user can create these templates on his own. There are several features for adapting the catalog to the company's needs, e.g. inserting manual pages, page breaks or references.

Some PIM features are supported to a lesser extent. Units can be created in MeDaPro but automatic conversion is not supported out-of-the-box. Likewise, price calculation in the PIM system. ITB feels that this can be done better in other systems. ConnectPro however makes it possible to get prices from the ERP system on the fly. Similarly, Product Lifecycle Management should, according to ITB, not be the task of a PIM system but of another specialized software system.

ConnectPro is, compared with some other PIM offerings, more extensive. It allows the user to create his own mapping in a graphical intuitive interface. Likewise, various import formats are offered for Excel, Access, CSV, BMEcat and ERP systems (SAP, Navision, Axapta, Dynamics, ProAlpha, alphaplan, Sage, and many more). Several standard classification systems are supported like eClass, ETIM, Proficlass, UNSPSC and EAN.

Finally, ITB offers the following goodies:
- iPad Catalog solution with ordering functionality;
- FlipCatalog, online PDF catalog to flip through with connection to the shop;
- Multichannel Connector to connect the PIM to platforms, e.g. Amazon, or other partners.

9.9.3   Technical Overview

The platform is based on the .Net framework and uses MS SQL.

9.9.4   Why Consider?

ITB positions itself not as a PIM-only specialist. It offers a very broad solution covering not only PIM but also a Web shop and interface tooling. All three components have grown through the years in parallel. The price structure makes the complete offering attractive for medium-sized companies.

References	
Wholesale	Reiff TP Technische Produkte GmbH, Uwe Kloska GmbH, Schrauben-Jäger AG, WS Weinmann & Schanz GmbH
Production	P. J. Dahlhausen & Co., BP Bierbaum-Proenen, Heinrich Schmidt, Detering, ISG, Leysser, Fuchs-Movesa, Paul Lange & Co.

9.10   Oracle Corporation

Sachin Patel, Product Strategy Director

9.10.1   The Company

With more than 390,000 customers, including 100 in the Fortune 100, and with deployments across a wide variety of industries in more than 145 countries around the globe, Oracle offers a huge stack of business hardware and software systems.

Key facts	
Founded	1977
Employees	120,000
Customers	390,000 (overall)
Main industries	Overall: communications, construction, education, financial services, life sciences and healthcare, manufacturing, professional services, public sector, retail
Turnover (2012)	US$37.1 billion
Net income (2012)	19.92 billion
Solution	SAAS, hosted and on premises
License structure	Not published

Oracle's product information management solution, called Product Hub, is a pre-built product master data management application as opposed to a toolkit that some vendors offer in the market. Oracle customers get the benefit of a robust data model that has evolved over 25 years supporting the needs of a variety of industries.

Oracle's Product Hub is part of the multi-domain portfolio of Master Data Management Applications include Customer, Supplier, Site and Hierarchy Management.

An additional unique selling point is Oracle's Enterprise Data Quality solutions that are pre-integrated with our Master Data Management solutions providing proactive and pervasive data quality.

Oracle's PIM system is built on the latest open standards Fusion Middleware Technology platform that leverages rich data integration, database, content management and workflow services directly in the applications.

9.10.2 Proposition

Oracle Product Hub has a pre-packaged yet easily extensible data model that allows customers to store any kind of structured and unstructured product data. Customers can use a rich set of seeded attributes or define their own.

The platform provides full category and classification management capabilities. Customers can define their own category hierarchies for different business purposes including Web navigation/e-commerce, merchandising, financial reporting, industry classifications such as UNSPSC.

PIM process	
Master data management	V
Category management	V
Classification and attribute management	V
Unit management	V
Catalog management	V
Data quality management	V
Product lifecycle management	V
Publication management	V
Product localization	V
Authorization management	V
PIM 2 Print support	Ext.
Media asset management	V
Workflow management	V
Price management	V
Product enrichment	V
Mass mutations and rollback	V

Data stewards have the ability to assign items individually or in bulk to one or more categories at any level in the hierarchy. They have multiple methods of accomplishing this including Excel or direct updates through the UI. They can also leverage real time data quality to automatically assign items to different categories based on attributes and descriptions. Customers also have the ability to publish their category hierarchies in different formats including HTML, PDF, RTF and Excel based on user configured templates.

The Oracle Product Hub gives customers the ability to define their custom units of measure and conversions between units.

Customers can define catalogs containing multiple category hierarchies and associate items at different levels of the hierarchy. Different attachments, including images, repository files and URLs, can be associated to a catalog. Oracle Product Hub makes it possible to share items and categories across catalogs so they can be maintained centrally and re-used in different catalogs. It also provides catalog category mapping so categories in one catalog can be mapped to other categories in different catalogs.

Data quality is one of the strengths of the Oracle Product Hub. It provides embedded governance analytics as well as real-time data quality with its out-of-the-box integration with Oracle Enterprise Data Quality for Product Data. For example, data stewards can monitor approved/rejected items by item class or assess the completion cycle times of high priority change orders. Oracle also provides granular security control to enforce data restrictions and robust collaborative workflows to orchestrate the review and approval of product data across the enterprise.

Oracle Product Hub natively provides Design, Pre-Production/Prototype, Production, and Obsolete phase types along with the ability for business users to easily define their own lifecycle phases and associated business rules. For example, customers can enforce certain attributes to be filled in before a product can move from design to production phase. Customers also have the ability to enforce different change policies for different lifecycle phases of a product.

Customers have various options for publishing items, item structures, catalogs and metadata configurations (including item class and value set setups) to multiple consuming systems synchronously or asynchronously. Publication options include a set of standard APIs, Web Services and ETL tools that enable the export of files in various file formats including XML, Excel and CSV.

Role Based security gives customers the ability to restrict access based on roles. Customers can also enforce more granular security including the ability to restrict access at the item class, item, organization and attribute group levels. Furthermore, customers can also define their own custom roles for their business needs and give them the appropriate access rights and privileges to manage different aspects of product data.

Customers can associate media assets including images, videos, PDFs, .doc, Excel, and other formats to one or more products. Customers can categorize media assets. The association of media assets to products can be orchestrated through a workflow for a collaborative definition and approval. Oracle Product Hub provides tools to manage digital assets including the ability to check-in/check-out files and maintain version history.

Oracle Product Hub provides a flexible and extensible workflow management framework that allows customers to define their own workflows. With the embedded analytics that comes with Oracle Product Hub, data stewards can monitor the definition, approval and overall completion cycle times of workflows.

Oracle Product Hub makes it possible for customers to manage various aspects of pricing. In addition, customers can easily define their own pricing attributes within minutes and write business rules to define pricing relationships.

Product Managers are able to perform mass updates directly from the UI as well as through Excel. Rollbacks are managed through item versions.

Oracle Product Hub provides standards-based integration options to import/export product data synchronously or asynchronously. A rich set of Java APIs and public Web services allow real-time synchronization of product data with other systems. CSV, Excel and XML based uploads to staging tables allow batch-based import of product data. Data stewards can also review product data, perform data quality checks and ensure data accuracy prior to importing data into the hub. As part of the data quality check, customers can de-duplicate, auto classify and standardize product data. On the outbound side, customers are able to export product and catalog information in various formats. Catalogs can be exported in HTML, PDF, RTF, Excel and other common file formats. Customers can also use ETL tools such as Oracle Data Integrator to publish item information from Oracle Product Hub to other systems in their enterprise. The integration features can also be used to support external PIM to Print applications.

9.10.3 Technical Overview

Oracle's Product Hub system is based on PL/SQL, Java and Oracle Database. It is built on a open standards based Fusion Middleware Technology Platform.

Standard interfaces supported include: Agile PLM, Oracle E-Business Suite, Siebel, Retek, Oracle Bills and Revenue Management.

Oracle's Product Hub has a pre-built data model that provides key entities to support product information and definition use-cases such as Attributes, Catalogs, Item Relationships, Product Taxonomy, Product Structure.

In addition to the data model, Oracle's solution also provides a business user configuration of metadata as opposed to an IT involved customization approach. From an Architecture standpoint it also provides embedded and configurable workflow, intelligence, content management and rich APIs and Web services for both onboarding and publishing of product content from the Product Hub. It also has an embedded Rules engine allowing customers to define custom business validation logic.

9.10.4 Why Consider?

Oracle does not publicly share its product roadmap unless a non-disclosure agreement is signed. But at a broad level Oracle's Product Hub solution focuses on providing integrated Product Information Management to support the Multi Channel Commerce in conjunction with best in class assets Oracle has acquired in this space.

References	
Manufacturing	Boeing, Sherwin Williams
Catering	Red Robin
Media	O'Reilly Media
Retail	Petco, Tesco
Wholesale	C & S Whole Grocers, HD Supply
Technology	Cisco, Dell

Oracle's product hub is extensive and a logical choice for companies who have already standardized on the Oracle platform. For newcomers its pre-package data model and advanced data quality features can be very interesting for a fast start and migration.

9.11   Riversand Technologies

Upen Varanasi, CEO and Co-Founder

9.11.1 The Company

Riversand was founded in 2001. If focuses on global players seeking comprehensive and cost-effective PIM and MDM solutions.

The company wants to be a knowledgeable, strategic partner for companies wanting to improve their entire product information supply chain, whether the needs are in supplier-facing activities such as engineering and procurement, or customer-facing interactions across multiple channels and markets.

Key facts	
Founded	2001
Employees	165
Customers	52
Main industries	Retail, Distribution, Health/Pharma, Manufacturing, Energy
Turnover (2010/11)	Approximately $15 million (growing by 50 %/year)
EBIT	Approximately $6 million
Net income	Approximately $4 million
Solution	Web-based, on-premises or on-demand (SaaS)
License structure	Priced per user and entity record

Riversand focuses on companies in the Retail, Manufacturing, Distribution, Healthcare, Pharmaceutical and Energy sectors and works with various sized companies from SME to global organizations.

The company has four offices in the United States (Houston, Dallas, Boston, Miami), two in Europe (Munich, Zurich) and two in Asia (Bangalore, Mysore).

Riversand implements its own solution itself in the United States. Internationally, it has set up a network of system Integrators (e.g. Cap Gemini, Infosys, Accenture, etc.) to serve local and global customers in Europe, South America and Asia.

9.11.2 Proposition

Riversand's MDM Solution, MDMCenter was first released in 2001 and is currently on Version 7.2. All modules including the MDM, workflow, digital asset management and data quality solutions have been developed using the same data model and application framework.

PIM process	
Master data management	V
Category management	V
Classification and attribute management	V
Unit management	V
Catalog management	V
Data quality management	V
Product lifecycle management	P
Publication management	V
Product localization	V
Authorization management	V
PIM 2 Print support	V
Media asset management	V
Workflow management	V
Price management	V
Product enrichment	V
Mass mutations and rollback	V

The Riversand taxonomy management framework enables users to create their own data models. Standard features include:
- Classification of products into hierarchies and categories;
- Defining attributes and customizing them at category level;
- Create 'many-to-many' relationships between suppliers, internal business units and customers;
- Create multiple taxonomies to meet each individual business unit requirements;
- Support for industry standard classification classes.
- Etc.

MDMCenter's Catalog Management module enables data stewards to introduce new items and update item attributes in multiple catalogs, allowing them to develop product catalogs by region, product line or customer while re-using data models, values and product relationships such as cross-sell, up-sell, bill-of-material across catalogs.

Other standard PIM processes like Unit Management, Mass mutations and Rollback are also extensively supported.

MDMCenter may include advanced pricing information, including complex attributes to model graduated pricing models. Derived attributes such as margin, gross price calculation and shipping costs can be calculated automatically in the system. Price history (with rollback capability) is stored in the system for each product. MDMCenter also integrates with advanced pricing engines for more advanced capabilities such as dynamic and customer specific price management.

Riversand has a strong focus on data quality. A differentiator of MDMCenter in managing data quality is its level of integration across all different modules. MDMCenter's Attribute Management and Attribute Editor capabilities allow the user to define metadata requirements and validation rules for each instance of an attribute in the data model. This not only includes common restrictions like mandatory fields but also length restrictions, precision, etc. Validation can be done in real-time as users enter data. All validation rules can be conditionally applied based on category, user, type of item, catalog, workflow, etc.

MDMCenter's Data Quality Management (DQM) module offers data cleansing, normalization, enrichment, classification, data review and quality checking capabilities. The reporting module supports several out-of-the-box reports for improving data quality, such as orphan/omission/incomplete data checking, duplicate Identification, advanced matching and identity resolution, data staging, exception reporting and a DQ dashboards.

Riversand offers several additional tools for data validation and data quality. The data aggregation module provides data validation checks as data is pulled from other systems. Riversand's data syndication module can perform checks before data is sent to subscribing systems. Errors can also kick-off a workflow to ensure proper corrective measures are taken. And at any point, datasets can be analyzed and data quality reports generated (to communicate to vendors how data conforms to standards, for instance). In addition to the systems own reports, data can be exported to BI systems such as Microstrategy, Cognos and others for inclusion in company-wide analytics and reports.

Both MDMCenter's user interface and data model support multiple languages and differentiates among locales and/or dialects (for instance, Brazilian Portuguese versus native Portuguese or Canadian French versus native French). The MDM Solution comes with over 140 major locales preloaded in the system and new languages/locales can easily be added. Localization is also supported for units of measure, currencies, attributes, etc. MDMCenter ships with Google translation integration but Riversand also has a partnership with Across Systems for intelligent translation services.

MDMCenter's aggregation module provides a management cockpit for easy creation and use of data formatters to syndicate and provide data in formats required by external systems. Formats have been developed for ERP systems, BI tools, CRM packages, Print Publishing applications, third-party MAM systems, Data Warehouses, e-commerce platforms, WMS, etc via Web services, Remote Function Calls, message queues and automated file import/exports (FTP) in different formats like CSV, Excel and other text-based delimited files.

MDMCenter's publishing solution enables bi-directional synchronization and output of product information and templates to a number of third party publishing solutions including Quark Xpress and Adobe InDesign and other file formats including HTML, .pdf, Word and PowerPoint.

9.11.3 Technical Overview

MDMCenter is a Web-based MDM solution based on the Microsoft platform including Windows Server, SQLServer, and .NET.

9.11.4 Why Consider?

Riversand is a pure-play MDM/PIM solution provider. Its core is the MDM/PIM area. For retailers and distributors Riversand has invested strongly in a distributor portal, workflow and data quality to allow the efficient handling of hundreds of thousands of products. It supports many industry standard supports like UNSPSC, eCl@ss, NRF ARTS, 1Worldsync, etc.

References	
Retail	Bed Bath & Beyond, Nordstrom, Overstock.com, Topco, etc.
Manufacturing	Siemens, Saint-Gobain, Liebherr, etc.
Distribution	ScanSource, PC Connection, Weatherford, Halliburton, etc.
Health/Pharma	GHX, Teva Pharmaceuticals
Energy	ConocoPhillips, ExxonMobil, Spectra Energy, etc.

With its own consultancy services the company not only helps with software implementation but also with achieving the business goals of the customer by focusing on gaining a high ROI while reducing the Total Cost of Ownership. In addition, Riversand also partners with an extensive network of global system integrators to augment its implementation teams.

9.12 Stibo Systems

9.12.1 The Company

Stibo's parent company, Stibo A/S, was founded in 1794 to serve the Royal House of Denmark and is still privately held.

Key facts	
Founded	1794/1976
Employees	230
Customers	200+
Main industries	Manufacturing, retail, distribution, leisure
Turnover (2010/11)	Not published
EBIT	Profitable since 2004 with double digit CAGR in the same period
Net income	Not published
Solution	Rich client and Web based. Hosted on site (at customer or at Stibo)
License structure	Based on number of users, volume and modules

Stibo A/S is a foundation whose charter is to ensure the long-term development of the company and contribute to the community. Since 1965, all company profits have been reinvested in the business and in charitable organizations worldwide.

As a result Stibo Systems, which was founded in 1976, can be considered the oldest PIM supplier covered in this book. The subsidiary company offers MDM/PIM solutions for (global) manufacturing, distribution, retail, travel and hospitality, automotive, and grocery companies.

Stibo Systems is headquartered in Denmark and has offices in the USA, Canada, UK, Germany, Sweden, France, Switzerland, India, Singapore, Netherlands, Australia, and Brazil. Istsells in China, Japan, Argentina and Chile through resellers and agents.

Key technology partners are Adobe, Quark, Microsoft, Oracle and IBM. Companies that offer integration services include Accenture, Deloitte, Cap Gemini and Sapient.

9.12.2 Proposition

STEP is the name of Stibo's PIM/MDM/DAM software platform. On top of the platform, STEP adds a suite of integrations for typical business uses like print, pricing, sales support, translation management etc.

PIM process	
Master data management	V
Category management	V
Classification and attribute management	V

(continued)

Unit management	V
Catalog management	V
Data quality management	V
Product lifecycle management	V
Publication management	V
Product localization	V
Authorization management	V
PIM 2 Print support	V
Media asset management	V
Workflow management	V
Price management	V
Product enrichment	V
Mass mutations and rollback	V

The way STEP allows the definition of business-specific logical data models is by using a generalized object-oriented data modeling (products, locations, suppliers, customers, etc.) architecture. Data models can be defined directly in the STEP GUI or imported without requiring system downtime. Business entities can be hierarchy specific or available to multiple hierarchies. Data and metadata are held in attributes that are defined independently, and can be shared between object types. The attribute definition holds basic field-level business logic associated with data validation, data types, input masks, valid units of measure.

Pricing information in STEP is managed in commercial lists. Commercial list data consists of terms. A term for a product is a combination of a value i.e. price and a set of conditions such as minimum quantity, maximum quantity, start date and end date. A product can be incorporated within multiple commercial lists thus enabling an item to have multiple prices.

STEP provides an embedded Data Quality module, which supports information quality management at various states of the data lifecycle. When importing data from external parties or feeds from other systems, STEP provides features for harmonizing and cleansing the data as well as matching and merging according to pre-defined rules. All rules are configured within the STEP GUI using tools for data profiling, previewing, look-up table definitions, and extensible normalization rule libraries. Adaptive improvement of rules is supported by routing erroneous data-feed subsets to error queues. Data stewards can then create or modify rules to either handle the error or ignore it so the same error will not occur again.

STEP Workflow includes workflow status reports, including user task assignments, objects in workflows and task completion times. STEP Workflow can be integrated into other business systems using the STEP Server SDK. The description of a workflow is achieved using the XML format called "State Chart XML" (SCXML), which is a standard developed by the W3 organization. Based on the workflow engine, workflows can be defined such as multi-user approval processes where privileged users can approve specific data only.

The STEP Information Server provides business users with overviews of the status of product data within the STEP system including products with missing digital assets, inconsistent and/or missing pricing, attributes values, references etc. An interface is offered for the creation of custom reports using third-party business intelligence (BI) tools such as SAP Business Objects, IBM Cognos, MicroStrategy or SAS Business Intelligence.

STEPS Audit Trail allows users to see who touched an item, when and what was changed. An Excel-like grid allows users to put multiple versions of content side by side and turn on a "Mark Different" view which highlights changes to the item over time. Rollbacks and purges are supported. The audit trail tracking extends to include the supplier users.

Localization can combine multiple dimensions such as market, language and channel. Native support for Unicode is offered to manage languages like Russian, Japanese, Chinese and Korean. Inbuilt processes are offered which automatically identify data that requires new translation or re-translation, either on-line or off-line. Integration with several external translation memory applications is supported.

Using STEP Proof View business users can automatically create previews to see how product information will look when published to different channels. Previews can be generated to show Web pages, shelf edge labels, point of sale signage, promotional flyers, packaging design, etc.

It is possible with STEP bulk updater to update a collection of objects in order e.g. to set an attribute value or introduce a new reference. STEP Excel Portal allows a user to export products to Microsoft Excel. Editing products in Excel is equivalent to editing them in STEP. The same attributes and attribute validations (number, text, list of value, etc.) and the same requirements (required or read only) will be enforced. When the user has finished editing the products, the Excel document is uploaded to STEP.

STEP Import and Export Manager enables users to upload files in a number of formats including CSV, Excel, STEPXML, generic XML and industry standards such as BMEcat and SAP IDOC. ETL features are offered for harmonization, data cleansing, record matching, mapping, validation and conversion. Import and export templates can be saved for easy ad hoc re-use and scheduled to happen on a regular basis.

STEP supports PIM to print with, among others things, a plug-in for Adobe InDesign. STEP Flat Planner is a digital whiteboard that enables the user to create a plan for a page or spread. Content can be dragged and dropped onto the plan, dragged to position and allocated space. InDesign Server automatically generates a preview of the page for review. Flat Planner also incorporates an analytics component that can display sales data, square inch information, and calculated information around the sales effectiveness of printed publications.

STEP Promotion Planner provides an integrated advertising, marketing and merchandising toolset that supports the collaborative planning, management and execution of versioned promotional offers including Free Standing Inserts (FSI) and retail store specific promotional flyers. This, for example, allows merchandisers to define pricing rules for offers that vary across store price zones, e.g. reducing the price by 20 % for stores that are close to a competitor but only by 10 % for stores that are not.

Stibo plans to continue to invest in what they call the "Information Supply Chain". STEP functionality and underlying technology is updated via monthly patch releases and a major new release every 12–18 months. Customers are encouraged to contribute ideas to the product development team through the Customer Portal, at regular customer conferences, and through the Customer Advisory Board. For 2013 Stibo plans to improve and/or expand, among other things, distributed data integration, social media and CRM adapters, BI Integration, affiliate feeds, automated classification and advanced data quality management.

9.12.3 Technical Overview

The core STEP system is developed in Java. The STEP Web Services API allows for STEP components to be developed in other languages such as C#, VB.net, C++ capable of calling Web Services. STEP runs on an Oracle database and Windows 2008R2 or Redhat Enterprise Linux operating system.

Interfaces to several middleware systems are supported like JMS queues, IBM WebSphere MQ, Oracle Advanced Queuing (AQ) and SAP MATMAS IDOC. Likewise, plug-ins are available to the major e-commerce systems like Oracle ATG Commerce, IBM WebSphere Commerce Server, hybris and Demandware.

9.12.4 Why Consider?

Stibo supports all the major PIM processes and offers an impressive list of modules and extensions. It has focused on improving the core PIM processes by optimizing data integration, quality management and distribution to the max while offering many system interfaces and options to cover related processes in the area of print and e-commerce.

References	
Retail	Bol.com, Toys 'R 'Us, Sears
Distribution	Grainger, VWR International, Barnes Distribution
Manufacturing	Kellogg, Philips, Fujitsu, Sony, Siemens
Other	Thomas Cook, Mitchell & Butlers

On top of this Stibo's STEP system is not limited to a PIM system, it is a multi-domain MDM solution that provides not only with a single view of all product and supplier information but also of location, customer and other types of master data that drive your business. As a result, Stibo is a solution considered by many global corporate companies.

9.13 SynchForce

Hans de Gier and Hans van den Berg, Owners

9.13.1 The Company

SyncForce, based in the Netherlands, believes that only strong brands will survive. Strong brands must offer a distinctive and consistent brand experience across all customer touch points.

Key facts	
Founded	1999
Employees	25
Customers	72
Main industries	FMCG, Construction and Pharma
Turnover	Not public
EBIT	Not public
Net income	Not public
Solution	SAAS only
License structure	Subscriptions starting at 1,465 € per month

To support these brands SyncForce offers an integral brand management platform that allows product development, marketing and sales to jointly develop all touch points based on a shared brand strategy and shared brand DNA.

The platform is used by 72 primarily larger companies mainly in the construction, FMCG, and pharma industries, but also automotive, retail and agriculture sectors. In total 35,000 marketing and sales professionals in 158 countries use the SAAS based platform.

SyncForce both serves customers directly and via implementation partners and VARs. SyncForce is privately owned by the two founders.

9.13.2 Proposition

The company's platform offers a central source for all brand-related guidelines, product information, promotional materials and media.

PIM process	
Master data management	V
Category management	V
Classification and attribute management	V
Unit management	V

(continued)

Catalog management	V
Data quality management	V
Product lifecycle management	V
Publication management	V
Product localization	V
Authorization management	P
PIM 2 Print support	V
Media asset management	V
Workflow management	P
Price management	V
Product enrichment	V
Mass mutations and rollback	V

All major PIM processes are supported: product enhancement, category management, classification and attribute management, etc.

A DAM module is part of the overall solution to store all digital and promotional assets. Quality management is supported by several data quality check reports.

Where SyncForce distinguishes itself is the extensive support of product lifecycle management. Where most PIM packages only support a product state, SyncForce supports NPD (New Product Development) and EPD (Existing Product Development) project management functionality.

Publication management is also supported widely. Standard Web services (XML) are offered but also database publishing services (Doc, PDF, InDesign) and exports (XLS, CSV, XML).

Price management is partly offered. Gross-price calculation is not supported (can only be stored). However, price history on different price levels is offered including support for customer specific pricing. Price promotion mechanisms are also supported (e.g. buy X get Y for free, X % discount on all products in category Y, etc.).

SyncForce does not offer ETL-based tools but has integrations with all major ERP systems (SAP, Oracle MS Dynamics, Infor, etc.). The platform also supports several external classification models like ETIM, GS1, GPC and PS in Foodservice.

Due to its focus and vision, SyncForce also supports processes rarely or not seen in other solutions like Channel Partner Relationship Management, Marketing Activity Management, Success Story Management (reference projects) and Event Planning.

Improvements are planned in 2013 for those areas in which SyncForce is still weak e.g. Workflow and Authorization Management, which will be expanded from product level to attribute level. Workflow features will be expanded to better support translation processes.

SyncForce also plans several new extensions for 2013, including a B2B Commerce module, a new product launch module with connectors to Social Media and an approval module for packaging and other artwork designs.

9.13.3 Technical Overview

The SyncForce platform is based on Microsoft .Net, SQL Server and Adobe InDesign. No third party solutions are used in the platform.

The solution is fully cloud-based (single instance, multi-tenant) with new features added every 2 weeks for all users.

9.13.4 Why Consider?

SyncForce is not a hardcore MDM/PIM software developer. The solution has a cross-functional focus covering the R&D, product management and marketing department related processes. SyncForce supports not only the core PIM processes but also project management for product development and marketing processes for campaign management and publication.

References	
Construction	CRH, Bolton Group, Wavin, Stanley Black & Decker, etc.
FMCG	Reckitt Benckiser, Bavaria, Princess, Pepsico, etc.
Pharma	Boehringer Ingelheim, Mediq, Astellas, etc.

About Unic

The Unic team is delighted to have been able to contribute its expertise to the production of this book.

Unic is a leading supplier of premium e-business solutions in Europe. The Swiss e-business provider offers integrated solutions from one source for e-commerce, digital communication and collaboration. In order to achieve this, Unic's competences in consulting, creation, implementation and operations are combined.

Unic was founded in 1996 and currently has a presence in three countries. Over 220 Unic employees work in Bern, Karlsruhe, Munich, Vienna and Zurich on successful e-business solutions for B2B and B2C markets, with the aim of maximizing the market success of their customers on a long-term basis. The staff at Unic draw from a broad range of expertise, excellent methodological skills and many years of project experience in all aspects of e-business.

Unic's Web and mobile solutions are based on enterprise software from market-leading partners. Its innovative approach is tailored in both concept and technology to individual business strategies and the technical requirements of the client.

Unic not only has extensive experience and references in product information management and e-commerce, it is also your partner for related areas such as information design, usability, e-marketing, Web analytics, SEO/SEM and hosting. Technically complex solutions integrated with various peripheral systems have been implemented successfully in numerous projects.

Unic's unique selling proposition is based on quality, commitment, expertise and sustainability. It draws on extensive experience from more than 1,500 projects implemented in close collaboration with its partners, many of which are featured in this book.

J. Abraham, *Product Information Management*, Management for Professionals,   177
DOI 10.1007/978-3-319-04885-7, © Springer International Publishing Switzerland 2014

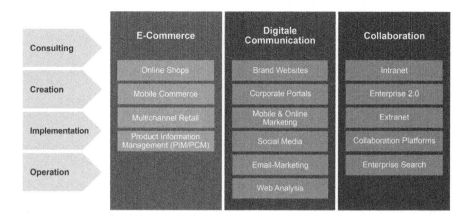

Integrated solutions from one source

Selected clients include Audi, Bridgestone, Caritas, Calida, Coca-Cola, Credit Suisse, Die Schweizerische Post, Galeries Lafayette, HORNBACH, JURA, Kistler, Manor, ÖBB, Palfinger, PKZ, SBB, Swisscom, UBS, University of St. Gallen (HSG), Victorinox, and Zurich Insurance Group.

Unic looks forward to supporting the implementation of your e-business projects. For more information, please visit http://www.unic.com.

About the Author

Jorij Abraham is founder of the E-commerce Foundation, a non-profit organization dedicated to helping organizations and industries improve their e-commerce activities. He advises companies on e-commerce strategy, omnichannel development and product information management.

Jorij has focused his career on e-commerce and the business side of product information management. While writing part of this book he was Director of Consulting at Unic. He has in the past been e-commerce manager for several organizations including the Bijenkorf, a Dutch high-end department store chain, and TUI, Europe's largest travel organization. He was online publisher for Food & Travel at Sanoma Media, Benelux' largest print and online media company.

Jorij is currently Research & Advice Director at E-commerce Europe, an industry association representing the interests of over 4,000 companies in 13 European countries selling products via digital means.

Jorij lives happily with his wife and two sons in Duivendrecht, a small suburb of Amsterdam, the Netherlands.

Feel free to contact Jorij at any time on:
LinkedIn   nl.linkedin.com/in/jorijabraham
Email   jorij@abraham.net

J. Abraham, *Product Information Management*, Management for Professionals, 179
DOI 10.1007/978-3-319-04885-7, © Springer International Publishing Switzerland 2014